GLOBAL PERSPECTIVES

NAVEED QAZI

ISBN 13: 9798623667700

Proofreading, cover design, editing and formatting done by the author.

Typeset in Adobe Caslon Pro

www.naveedqazi.com

Paperback and digital edition available from Kindle Direct Publishing, an Amazon unit.

UK | US | Australia | Italy | Spain | India | Netherlands | Japan | Brazil | Canada | Germany | Mexico | UAE | Singapore | Turkey | Poland | China | Saudi Arabia

kindle
direct
publishing

ABBREVIATIONS

BGRIMM Beijing General Research Institute of Mining & Metallurgy
BOC Bank of China
BRICS Brazil Russia India China South Africa
BANDES *Banco de Desarrollo Económico y Social de Venezuela (Spanish)*
CADF China – Africa Development Fund
COMPLANT China Complete Plant Import and Export Corporation
COVEC China National Overseas Engineering Corporation
CCTV China Central Television
CALF China International Cooperation Company for Agriculture, Livestock and Fisheries
CCB China Construction Bank
CCE *Comercio de Componentes Electronicos (Portuguese)*
CELAC Community of Latin American and Caribbean States
CCT Conditional Cash Transfers
CIA Central Intelligence Agency
CDB China Development Bank
CHEXIM China Export Import Bank
CNPC China National Petroleum Corporation
CNOOC China National Offshore Oil Corporation
CNMC China Non-Ferrous Metals Cooperation
CHINALCO Aluminium Corporation of China
DAC Development Assistance Committee
EITI Extractive Industries Transparency Initiative
ECLAC Economic Commission for Latin America and the Caribbean
FATA Federally Administered Tribal Areas

FEES Economic and Social Stabilisation Fund
FDI Foreign Direct Investment
FOCAC Forum on China –Africa Cooperation
FCCV *Fondo Conjunto Chino Venezolano (Spanish)*
GBP Great Britain Pounds
GDP Gross Domestic Product
IEC Independent Election Committee
ICBC Industrial and Commercial Bank of China
IED Improvised Explosive Devices
IDB Inter-American Development Bank
ISIS Islamic State of Iraq & Syria
ISI Inter State Intelligence
IMF International Monetary Fund
IFI International Financial Institutions
KP Khyber Pakhtunwala
LT *Lashkar-e Toiba (Arabic)*
MEP Ministry of Environmental Protection
MQM *Muttahida Qaumi Movement (Urdu)*
NGOs Non-Governmental Organisations
NAFTA North Atlantic Free Trade Agreement
NATO North Atlantic Treaty Organisation
OECD Organisation for Economic Cooperation and Development
PBOC Peoples Bank of China
PAE Pan American Energy
R&D Research and Development
RAF Royal Air Force
RAW Research and Analysis Wing
SINOPEC China Petroleum and Chemical Corporation
SME Small Medium Enterprises
SINOPEC China Petroleum and Chemical Corporation
SEWA Self-Employed Women's Association
TTP *Tehrik-e Taliban Pakistan (Urdu)*
UNCDF United Nations Capital Development Fund
UN United Nations
US United States

CONTENTS

CHINESE ORDER

BELT AND ROAD

When one thinks of a geopolitical road initiative such as the Belt and Road, romantic images of the Silk Road, Marco Polo's adventures, or Genghis Khan's empire come into mind.

In the past, Chinese envoys, during the Han dynasty, often visited Central Asia on missions of peace and friendship. The idea also represents those Western classical novels, where all disciplines, all sciences, and all forms of human activity are intertwined.

The Belt and Road, on the map, criss-crosses Eurasia, in all directions, including six economic corridors on land, and three sea routes, where the goal is to create a new global economy and place China at its centre.

The Eurasian trade, in goods, is now close to two trillion American dollars each year. It is more than double the volume of transatlantic trade, and significantly more than transpacific trade.

Whosoever controls and builds infrastructure, linking the two ends of Eurasia, will rule the world. China realises this, especially at a point in time, when Eurasia is becoming more integrated and has acquired a stage of intense rivalry and competition.

The Belt and Road is the Chinese plan to build a new world order, replacing the US-led international system.

If China succeeds in building a new world map, in front of our own eyes, it will very likely that we might use Belt and Road, as a new grouping, just as we use the term 'West' for the existing world order.

In this new world order, Beijing can project power over two-thirds of the world, including global public opinion. Most likely, it will limit other countries, as mere regional and parochial powers, to retain their sovereignty.

Wherever China finds little resistance or a vacuum, it will move in. And, wherever it finds resistance, it will stop. This new geopolitical and economic praxis, in other words, means that there is a slow, but the gradual expansion of Chinese influence.

Many things, in this movement, are uncertain, but the way Chinese leaders are approaching it is much closer to Lenin's philosophy than Marx's.

Belt and Road, will make China rise, at the centre stage, at an unprecedented level, affecting our fates, because at the end, a question will arise whether a new world order will be born, or will there be a status quo, or will there be a war between the United States and China. It was in 2015 when news started to reach the European cities that China was launching a new initiative.

Back then, it was termed as 'New Silk Road', consisting of number or railways routes, criss-crossing Central Asia's flat, un-forested lands, linking China and Europe, even though ships were seen as a better alternative to rails, for moving goods, in gigantic container ships, around the globe.

Economists, therefore, believed that China's perception of

replacing sea transportation with a new network of roads and railroads, across Central Asian forestlands, deserts, and mountains would not be economically viable. In 2016, Financial Times reported all rail transport, heading west from China, was eager to do their part for the New Silk Road initiative.

Many watchers, at that time, disdained the project, because its economic rationale, due to its sheer size, remained doubtful. But there were some arguments supporting the initiative as well.

The supporters of the project, however, believed that an interconnected system of transport, energy, and digital infrastructure, would gradually develop, into industrial clusters, and free trade zones, and then an economic corridor would get formed, consisting of construction, logistics, energy, manufacturing, agriculture, and tourism, giving birth to a large Eurasian common market trade.

At home, the project was called One Belt, One Road. The scope, set by its planners, was set to around thirty years, with the first phase of the project to be concluded in 2021, and the realisation of the whole project was done by 2049.

It connected the old Taoist wisdom, with postmodern cities, linking China's past and future. Thus, the project is often regarded as a dagger in the heart of the economic societies, in the West. It is because the project has the potential to bring many countries under its economic orbit, and ideological mindset.

Former White House Secretary of State, Rex Tillerson described Belt and Road initiative as a Faustian pact, where member countries sacrificed their ideals and independence on cheap loans. In south Asia, commentators think that the Belt and Road is a project of Chinese expansionism, but with a thinly disguised military element, as China is using a dual port system that berths cargo ships, and military vessels together.

China has already opened a military port, in Djibouti. Now, it has plans to open other similar ports in Sri Lanka and Pakistan.

***

The Belt and Road is also termed as a new and more active foreign policy strategy that is aimed at shaping China's external environments, rather than merely adapting to it.

As the United States perceives China, as a major threat, the external environment is ought to become more hostile, at a time, when China's economic growth is rising, and its insistence on placing certain demands on other countries.

A watershed movement arrived after the convening of the Working Conference, on Neighbourhood Policy, in October 2013, where President Xi Jing Ping, announced that China should be more active in promoting diplomacy, with its neighbours.

It was a bold departure from Deng's foreign policy, when 'striving for achievement' was given a preference over 'keeping a low profile.'

The initial impetus for Belt and Road is largely attributed to the success of Chinese industry, where the country's modernisation plan could be expanded, to other parts of the world. Firstly, starting with infrastructure, and then moving to manufacturing, China would get new markets for exports, but at the same time, it could no longer produce goods at home, which yielded no profits.

By controlling the pace, and structure of investments, China could have a transition to high-value manufacturing and services. It also meant that it could no longer rely on Western economies to provide a favourable environment.

In Belt and Road project, it seems, different policies can be pursued simultaneously, such as increasing connectively, to boost demands of Chinese aluminium and steel, but it can also be a way to establish newer energy routes, linking producers in Central Asia, and energy deficient Chinese cities and factories.

This strategy might become a priority for Chinese foreign policy. Hence, China needs to diversify its energy imports, by building new gas pipelines or expanding the network of ports and oil terminals.

Developing new technology in renewables will also benefit from the Belt and Road. By developing new trade and energy routes, the vulnerability of China to an American naval blockade of the Malacca strait, known as the 'Malacca Dilemma' can be avoided, in case of a conflict. In just a few years, China will need to import six hundred million tonnes of crude oil, and three hundred million cubic meters of natural gas annually. According to some estimates, the different continental corridors envisaged by the Belt and Road will provide up to one hundred forty-three million tonnes of crude oil and two hundred six billion cubic meters of natural gas.

Predictably, the Belt and Road also might further develop *renminbi*, as a global trade and investment currency, for its greater use in international transactions, especially related to energy development and investments in infrastructure.

Through the initiative, Chinese companies will make increasing amounts of overseas investment in *renminbi*, and the most fundraising. It might create spillover effects in other payment methods.

In October 2013, President Xi Jing Ping appealed to the spirit of the ancient Silk Road, the grid of trade routes, connecting civilisations in Asia, Europe, and Africa.

The Chinese Premier, therefore, had urged the world, to enter a new age. As the initiative had land and sea components known as Silk Road Economic Belt, and Twenty-First Century Maritime Silk Road, the preferred abbreviation came to be known as Belt and Road.

The Silk Road Economic Belt and the 21st Century Maritime Silk Road were officially endorsed by the Chinese Communist Party, after Xi's speeches in Astana and Jakarta.

However, it was not until 2015, that Belt and Road started to feature in the State Council's reports on government work, and strategy and planning documents.

Several countries had been made members of this initiative, but the list was never final or exclusive. Its maps today, which are known, are tentative, and mainly circulated by Xinhua, a Chinese news agency, which shows a line, passing from Xian to Istanbul.

In May 2015, Chinese media reported that there were over nine hundred major projects at the national level, already in the pipeline, of which fifty would be launched soon, and twenty were related to the Maritime Silk Road.

The initiative was also featured in China's thirteenth five-year plan, which outlines the country's key priorities, for 2016-20, and dedicates a separate chapter, to the aim of progressing with the Belt and Road initiative.

But whether this line represents a road or railway, remains unknown. However, as the line passes through conflict zones, such as Syria and Iraq, the whole idea raises more questions than answers.

Although, Xi Jing Ping noted that it is an economic belt of deeper integration, and not only a mere trade route. It has been organised into five different dimensions.

The first dimension is policy coordination. The second is transport infrastructure. The third is the removal of trade barriers. Fourth is currency integration. And, the fifth encourages more intense exchanges and contacts between people. In other words, Belt and Road defend the idea, that China's problems cannot be addressed in isolation, but with mutual association with other countries.

Therefore, this new political confidence speaks of global Chinese values, reducing the rise of Western cultural imperialism.

China plans to set up a new international court for settling disputes among companies participating in the Belt and Road. It is aimed to protect the legal rights of Chinese and foreign parties, for a transparent and stable environment, governed by a rule of law, with its headquarters based in Beijing. Hence, Belt and Road is meant to introduce a new theory in international relations that rejects power politics and is committed to settling disputes through dialogue, rather than confrontation.

Through Belt and Road, China will be organising and

leading global supply chains, reserving for itself the most valuable chains of production, and at the same time, creating strong relationships of collaboration and infrastructure with other countries, whose main role in the system would be to inherit lower value segments.

In this case, it owes some debt of inspiration to Mao's legacy, and Deng's vision of a world organised as a network of production chains. Although it does not intend to work as a geopolitical project, or as a project of intense rivalry, commentators believe that it might function as such, against China's wishes.

That is why the country is seeking to prioritise a win-win situation, when co-operation between two or more nations succeeds, and keeps the interests of everyone alive.

As China's economy grows in strength, the Belt and Road will get a push, which will give a new potential for attaining economic leverage.

Legally, or politically, the states would be fully sovereign and independent, but economic power would bind the member countries of Belt and Road together and would prevent it from failing or falling apart. This plan differs from existing Western orders, which emphasise legal and institutionalised procedures.

The Vision and Actions document describes the initiative 'to jointly build the Belt and Road' as 'aimed at promoting the orderly and free flow of economic factors, highly efficient allocation of resources, and deep integration of markets.' Simultaneously, it encourages 'the countries along Belt and Road to achieve economic policy co-ordination, and carry out broader, and more in-depth regional cooperation of higher standards.'

The document describes the government's central role as marshalling domestic resources, to provide stronger policy support, for the Belt and Road. It will facilitate the establishment of relevant financial institutions, and dedicated funds, and at the same time, provide the right financial regulation, to promote the initiative.

The initiative will abide by market rules, and international norms, and will play a decisive role in resource allocation in markets, and the primary role of the private sector, while letting government perform their functions.

Under the Chinese model, the state retains control over sectors, that are considered strategic, and it might be spread over to the Belt and Road initiative. For the internationalisation of state-owned enterprises, their preservation and growth, enterprises can engage in long-term investments abroad, because a lot of member countries need a massive number of investments in infrastructure, particularly, which cannot be easily undertaken by private enterprises.

The launch of Belt and Road might even propel the process of mergers and acquisitions, reflecting commitments to state capitalism, and its associate power relations.

Co-operation in infrastructure development could be a key step in facilitating the growth in trade, investment and economic development in China, and member countries, but it would also require policy co-ordination, and domestic efforts to lessen trade and investment barriers.

Thus, economic activity will get increased after proper connectivity, paving way for industrial parks, that will slowly integrate into regional value chains, and eventually support developed cities.

The different countries, along the Belt and Road, are said to have their resource advantages, where the ties that bind are primarily financial.

According to various estimates, the Belt and Road would require four trillion to eight trillion American dollars to realise its goals. Foreign direct investments and concessional loans make up the vast majority of Belt and Road financing. The terms of Chinese credit to countries along the Belt and Road vary widely, from interest-free loans, and grants, to fully commercial rates.

However, most of the member countries did not have the money to pay, for the projects, with which they were involved.

Many are heavily in debt and need sustainable finance and private investment. For example, in Sri Lanka, the government formally handed over the Hambantota port to China, in exchange for writing down the country's debt. Under a 1.1 billion American dollar deal, Chinese firms now hold a seventy per cent stake in the port, and a ninety-nine-year lease agreement to operate it.

***

Beijing regards financing mechanisms as a critical part of the initiative. It gives Belt and Road, a certain purpose, direction, and pace.

The Chinese state banks, Industrial and Commercial Bank of China, Agricultural Bank of China, Bank of China, and China Construction Bank will retain a certain role, but new financial institutions will also be created.

The Asian Infrastructure Investment Bank, founded on

December 25, 2015, with an authorised capital of around a hundred billion American dollars, considers Belt and Road a top priority. Thus, it approved five hundred nine million American dollars in investments for its first four projects, on June 25, 2016, on transportation, power, urban development, and other projects in Bangladesh and Tajikistan, all countries, under the core area of Belt and Road.

There is another development and investment fund called as The Silk Road Fund, established in Beijing, on December 29, 2014, with an investment of around forty billion American dollars, from the Chinese government's Foreign Exchange department, China Investment Corporation, Export-Import Bank of China, and China Development Bank. It focuses on investment opportunities and guides financing under the framework of Belt and Road.

After the detailed plans were set up in the Visions Document, China Development Bank, falling under the country's State Council, set up a project pool, involving nine hundred projects, from over sixty countries, in transportation, energy, resources, and other sectors.

In January 2018, Hu Huaibang, chairman of the bank, told that they had extended one hundred and ten billion American dollars, in loans, to projects along the ancient trade route, by the end of 2017, and announced plans for an additional two hundred and fifty billion American dollars.

Similarly, the Export-Import Bank of China started to focus on Belt and Road initiative in 2015. The bank planned to finance more than one thousand projects in forty-nine countries, covering transportation, electricity, resources, telecommunications, and industrial parks and has set up three co-operation funds, for investment in Belt and Road.

Industrial and Commercial Bank of China, the largest bank in the world, by assets, is taking part in the Belt and Road initiative, by investing in around two hundred and twelve projects, with credit facilities, exceeding sixty-seven billion American dollars.

However, the state-owned banking system remains a crucial instrument for managing development strategy, allowing credit to priority industries and projects, but the Chinese authorities, know that they run the risk of exercising too much control over investment decisions, at the expense of a more decentralised system for processing information.

***

On land, the Belt stretches from three routes, understood as broad geographical areas. One from Northwest China and Northeast China to Europe, and the Baltic Sea via Central Asia and Russia; one from Northwest China to the Persian Gulf, and the Mediterranean Sea, passing through Central Asia and West Asia, and one from Southwest China through Indochina Peninsula to the Indian Ocean.

These three routes are divided into six economic corridors connected by six means of communication.

The Belt and Road will focus on building a new Eurasian Land Bridge corridor and developing the China-Mongolia-Russia, China-Central Asia- West Asia and China-Indochina corridors by taking advantage of several transport routes and using key economic industrial parks as cooperation platforms.

The Vision and Action document describes the China-Pakistan Economic Corridor, and the Bangladesh-China-India-Myanmar Economic Corridor, as closely knit to the Belt and Road initiative.

It has been said that the China-Indochina corridor generally outperforms the other corridors. The China-West Asia corridor is the weakest of the six corridors, as many countries along the corridor belong to different economic groupings.

Unlike the original Silk Road, the Belt and Road is not predominantly about transport infrastructure, but also about economic integration.

Economic corridors are not mere transport connections, along which people and goods move, but they are rather complex economic geographies, taking advantage of specialisation, and connectivity, to bring superior and effective outcomes.

Hence, the idea behind Belt and Road is to create economic corridors by design, rather than letting them evolve naturally and slowly, on their own. And, these corridors require much more flow of future revenue.

***

China has been keen to construct high-speed railways outside its borders. Therefore, freight rail links have been built, expanded, and renovated in Uzbekistan, Kyrgyzstan, Pakistan, Kazakhstan and elsewhere. For quite a while, China has insisted on constructing a railway line connecting Kashgar in Xinjiang, to the Fergana valley, the core of Central Asian territory, through Osh in Kyrgyzstan, a project that could end century-old hostilities, and change the destiny of its plateaus.

New roads are already built in the region. Besides that, one of the most ambitious projects is the expansion of the Karakoram Highway linking Xinjiang to central Pakistan. Beijing has given one hundred fifty million American dollars, using a combination of grants and concessional loans, to upgrade a highway from Raikot to Thakot, in Khyber Pakhtunkhwa province.

A road realignment project is also under progress from Thakot to Havelian, in Khyber Pakhtunkhwa province, using a $1.3 billion concessional loan, that involves the construction of seven tunnels, and sixty-eight large bridges, that are aimed to get completed in 2020.

On the southern land route of Belt and Road, China plans to connect Southeast Asian countries, with the southwest region of Yunnan, through a series of high-speed railways.

There are three routes planned, a central one that runs through Laos, Thailand, and Malaysia, to reach Singapore; a western route through Myanmar, and an eastern one through Vietnam and Cambodia.

These projects are at various sources of development, with construction in the Thailand and Laos legs already progressing.

China is quickly planning several other overseas industrial development zones with good infrastructure, full access to public services, and giving rise to interconnected businesses.

In a 2016 progress report on the Belt and Road, eighteen border co-operation zones and fifty-two industrial parks, are being operational across eighteen countries. Some of the recent examples include the Horgos International Cooperation Centre, where goods are sold free of tariffs. In July 2018, a new financial hub opened in Astana called the Astana International Financial Centre, where Silk Road Fund and Shanghai Stock Exchange became shareholders.

Just across the border from Horgos, a major new dry port is being developed, with an ambition of connecting the Eurasian continent through a steady network of roads and railways. The plan will greatly benefit China, as they can enter the Russian market, without paying any duties.

China sees Kazakhstan as its gateway to Europe and has encouraged the speedy development of many of its Belt and Road projects there.

Of late, what has also worked for China is the integration of the Eurasian Economic Union with the Belt and Road. In May 2015, President Putin and Xi signed a joint statement on this matter. Commentators believe that Russia's nod to the project changed the parameters of Belt and Road.

It gave the green light to China's ambitions for countries such as Kazakhstan and Georgia, its gateways to Europe.

It was in May 2018 when China and Eurasian Economic Union signed a free trade agreement in Astana.

While tariffs were not cancelled, the agreement makes it possible to improve conditions for access of goods to the market through norms for trade facilitation and improve the level of interaction across all spheres of trade cooperation.

The other country where Belt and Road is making a big impact, just like in Kazakhstan, is Pakistan. Commentators believe that if Kazakhstan is China's gateway to Europe, Pakistan is the gateway to the Indian Ocean.

The strategic alliances between the two countries go back decades when it was expected that an economic corridor could be churned out starting from Kashgar in Xinjiang, and reaching Karachi and Gwadar.

China always has had an interest in Pakistan's vast internal market and its natural resources.

The China-Pakistan Economic Corridor is a development corridor covering the Xinjiang province, and the territory of Pakistan, covering Punjab, Sindh, Khyber Pakhtunkhwa, Balochistan, Azad Jammu and Kashmir, and Gilgit in Pakistan.

There are passages to several railways and highway trunk lines, from Islamabad to Karachi and Gwadar. Several sectors to be promoted in the corridor include textiles, production of parts and components for industry and agriculture.

There is also a plan to extract coal from the Thar Desert, which has one of the biggest deposits of lignite, a lower-grade brown version of fuel. The project also includes building power plants to expand capacity in the country that faces electricity shortages.

The first phase will add six hundred megawatts of power, and it can be scaled up to five thousand megawatts, to make it the largest cluster of electricity production in Pakistan. There is also a priority given to the construction and development of Gwadar city port. The project has attained a highly symbolic status for the Belt and Road. Gwadar lies in a privileged and strategical position. By becoming a new Chinese coastal city, it will link the western provinces of China to the Indian Ocean.

The port will have a new expressway, an international airport, an industrial park, and world-class tourism facilities. The industrial park provides foreign investors with a hundred per cent ownership, a twenty-three-year tax holiday, and an exemption from customs duties for the material used for the construction and operation of the port.

Today, more than a thousand people already work at the six-hundred-sixty-meter container terminal. A leading Chinese investment company announced that it would invest five hundred million, in the first phase of a project, aiming to build five hundred thousand homes for Chinese professionals, expected to be in Gwadar in 2023.

***

The Visions and Actions document proposed two routes for the Maritime Silk Road. The East route would start from China's coast through the South China Sea, to the South Pacific. The West route would travel through the South China Sea, and end in Africa and Europe.

The scheme was slightly modified in a 2017 vision document, entitled Vision for Maritime Cooperation, under the Belt and Road initiative, where three separate routes have been chalked out.

First, there is China - Indian Ocean - African -Mediterranean Sea Blue Economic Passage, linking the China-Indochina Peninsula Economic Corridor, and connecting the China-Pakistan Economic Corridor, and Bangladesh – China – India – Myanmar Economic Corridor.

Second, there is the 'blue economic passage' of China-Oceania-South Pacific, travelling southward from the South China Sea, into the Pacific Ocean. Another passage is also envisioned leading up to Europe via the Arctic Ocean.

China is willing to enhance customs cooperation, with countries along the Road, and to promote information exchange, mutual recognition of customs regulations, and mutual assistance in law enforcement.

As per Financial Times, nearly two-thirds of the world's container ports had received some degree of Chinese investment by 2015. During the first half of 2017, Chinese companies made plans to buy or invest in nine overseas ports, five of which are in the Indian Ocean.

Four separate initiatives are set for Malaysia, with Chinese company investments, scheduled for the $7.2 billion Melaka Gateway, the $2.84 billion Kuala Linggi Port, the $1.4 billion Penang Port, and the one hundred seventy-seven million American dollar Kuantan port projects.

For quite some time, Chinese companies have been involved in the construction, management, and expansion of Gwadar in Pakistan, Kyaukpyu in Myanmar, and Doraleh in Djibouti.

The first strategy includes hub ports, servicing huge

container ships, and transhipping them onto smaller vessels, to connect with regional ports.

The second strategy, as David Brewster, describes it, should not be overlooked and is perhaps more significant: ports such as Gwadar, and Kyaukpyu are meant to connect the Indian Ocean, with China via overland transport corridors. It is because Pakistan and Myanmar may become China's California, granting it access to a second ocean, and resolving the Malacca dilemma.

Having access to the Kyaukpyu project has always been a priority for China. The gas pipeline will carry up to twelve billion cubic meters of gas annually. It runs parallel to a Chinese pipeline with a capacity of twenty-two million barrels of oil per year, about six per cent of China's 2016 oil imports – it was built to transport oil, from the Middle East and Africa, directly to China, avoiding the Malacca Strait, and cutting distance by twelve thousand kilometres.

By using overland pipelines, connected to Gwadar, the result will be that it will reduce the distance from the Persian Gulf, to just two thousand five hundred kilometres, but the pipeline will depend on ultra-high power pumping stations, as it has to pass through the Karakoram pass, at an altitude of five thousand to six thousand meters, above Gwadar, or Kashgar.

On existing routes via the Malacca Strait, oil tankers need to travel more than twelve thousand kilometres, for two to three months, to reach China.

Hence, bypassing the Malacca Strait, by building a canal through Kra Isthmus in Thailand, around a hundred kilometres and twenty-five meters deep, would take ten years to build, but can be a game changer. From the shipping perspective, it could mean shorter and cheaper shipping times, perhaps two to three days faster shipping lanes for all.

However, it remains uncertain why Thailand would give a green signal to the project, as there is a growing Muslim insurgency in the south.

There are also reports of growing trade between India and China, in the future. Given their size, and proximity, the two countries are bound to develop the world's largest trading relationship. Therefore, it is not surprising that Kolkata features prominently, in the original plans for the Road, with the Indian city appearing on the famous map of the initiative, published by Xinhua.

The port could be an important place in developing value chains, and connecting Chinese and Indian manufacturers, but more recently, it has been dropped, from all official references, as India has recently distanced itself from the Belt and Road.

India's rejection of Belt and Road might have been triggered by the Doklam standoff. India also believes that the initiative will create unsustainable burdens of debt, and one of the economic corridors also passes through the disputed areas of Gilgit and Baltistan in Pakistan-occupied Kashmir, posing newer challenges.

There are also commentators, who believe that Belt and Road might force India, into newer forms of economic isolation. They believe that New Delhi may even see it as a form of rebuilding trade and economic links between Europe and Asia, while ignoring the Indian subcontinent, historically a meeting point for such trade and cultural networks.

Also, in January 2018, State Council Information Office published a white paper, titled 'China's Arctic Policy' whose main premise is that global warming will turn Arctic into a new area for economic activity, and state competition.

It is because, as ice melts, conditions for the development of Arctic may be gradually changed, opening opportunities for commercial use of sea routes, and the development of resources in the region.

There are rumours and predictions that Bering Strait will open for an extended period around 2020, the Northern Sea Route around 2025, and the Transpolar Route around 2030.

China is hoping to build a 'Polar Silk Road' along the Arctic shipping lanes, the third main sea route of the Belt and Road. The Arctic is gaining global significance, for its rising strategic, and economic values, and those relating to scientific research, environmental protection, sea passages, and natural resources.

Quite recently, it was said that shipping through the Northern Sea Route, would lessen twenty days off the regular passage time, using the traditional route through the Suez Canal.

In the media, it had been speculated lately that Maritime Silk Road is meant to build a new economic landscape, for the twenty-first century, as the official documents reveal the 'Ports-Park-City' model of development. For example, the Doraleh port, along the Maritime Silk Road, is a slowly expanding project, where China wants to move some of its low-end manufacturing, such as footwear, and apparel. For that purpose, it has financed and built a new fast railway linking Addis Ababa and Djibouti.

Maps of the Maritime Silk Road, released by the Chinese media, have shown the route running through the disputed areas in the South China Sea, a place of strategic rivalries.

Here, China is developing a confrontational foreign policy, where free and safe shipping lanes pass, as per information in the official document of Belt and Road. But commentators also argue that Belt and Road can bring new forms of co-operation, as Beijing is looking to end to open military conflict, through infrastructure development and economic means.

The Maritime Silk Road will advance Chinese interests, in many ways, in the South China Sea. Co-operation will help in reducing tensions. It can also strengthen institutional links, about maritime affairs.

Through the initiative, it can also avoid the involvement of outside actors, such as the United States.

However, with time, the dispute over land features and territorial waters, in the South China Sea, will shift in China's favour, once shipping lanes in the region will grow, and when Chinese companies, will start to dominate.

Majority of the ports could be controlled by China and have dual civilian and military uses.

A 2014 article in the Mandarin language Pacific Journal revealed China's Indian Ocean strategy. It called to select locations meticulously, make deployments discreetly, give priority to cooperate activities, and penetrate gradually.

The fact of the matter remains that for two decades, China

has been trying to extend its influence and activities, to the Indian Ocean. It has invested in ports in Sri Lanka, and Pakistan sent submarines across the Malacca Strait. The most dramatic instance of this overall development was the opening of the first military base in Djibouti, on the other side of the Indian Ocean. It is only Japan, which sees the Indian navy, as an indispensable partner, in its efforts, to contain Chinese expansion, and safeguards freedom of navigation, in the East and South China seas.

***

A priority identified in the Visions and Actions document is to improve the division of labour and distribution of industrial chains. When it comes to the division of labour along the value chains, of industrial production, positions, and preferences, that reflect the national interests of the countries, the regions of Belt and Road may differ, or even contradict each other.

Belt and Road, is the first of its kind policy, that has a transnational industrial policy. Services, too, have become so vital for global value chains, that increasing service exports will also be a strategic goal of the Belt and Road.

In the integrated framework of the Silk Road Economic Belt, new transport infrastructure could boost steel demand, and prepare the ground for China, to import steel from Central Asia, as it moves from higher value products, and value chain segments.

Soon, after the launch of the Belt and Road, Hebei Province, announced plans to move capacity for 5.2 million tons of steel, five million tons of cement, and three million units of glass abroad by 2018.

The targets for 2023 are even more ambitious, with a capacity of twenty million tons of steel, thirty million tons of cement, and ten million units of glass waiting to be relocated abroad. State-owned companies would help setup a six-hundred-thousand-ton steel project in Thailand.

In 2017, Tsingshan Group Holdings, a state back steel producer, based in Wenzhou on China's southeastern coast, opened two-million-ton stainless steel plant, on the Indonesian island of Sulawesi, which accounts for four per cent of the world's stainless-steel production.

Hence, the current production may find takers in Belt and Road countries, and at the same time will also help Chinese companies to stabilise the steel sector. Also, in other words, it means that if Belt and Road is to be understood as a form of transnational industrial policy, then China's industrial policy, cannot be considered independently.

That is why strategies like Made in China 2025, expand its focus to increase the global market share, by developing major industries and technologies of the future. International industrial capacity cooperation under the Belt and Road encompasses arrangements by which Chinese companies can also obtain technology from foreign entities.

What Belt and Road does is that it will increase China's control over the way value chains are organised, and grants it the power to reorganise them on better terms.

Hu Huaiberg, Chairman of the China Development Bank, has argued that the most important goal of the Belt and Road is to help China undergo economic structural reform, and upgrade its industries, which is moving away from a cheap, mass manufacturing model. It will help domestic industries that suffer from over-capacity problems.

***

Belt and Road in Pakistan is moving at a faster level. The plan has succeeded in a deep and broad penetration of almost all sectors of Pakistan's economy, by Chinese companies, and its wholesale reorganisation, to fit with Chinese-led value chains.

Chinese manufacturing enterprises relocate their factories to Pakistan, for low labour costs, and greater internationalisation.

At the same time, it also promotes the upgrade and reconstruction of the manufacturing industry in Pakistan, and creates many employment opportunities, for the local people.

A key element is a development of new industrial parks, surrounded by the necessary infrastructure, and a supporting policy environment. Chinese plans for Pakistan are focused on agriculture, and low-tech industry, encompassing entire value chains, including provisions of seeds and pesticides.

It includes the construction of one NPK fertiliser plant, as a starting point, with an annual output of eight hundred thousand tons. Meat processing plants in Sukkur are planned with an annual output of two hundred thousand tons per year, and two demonstration plants processing two hundred thousand tons of milk per year.

In crops, demonstration projects of more than six thousand five hundred acres will be set up for high-yield seeds, and irrigation, mostly in Punjab.
When it comes to transport and storage, the plan aims

to build a nationwide logistics network, enlarge the warehousing and distribution network, and enlarge the warehousing and distribution network between major cities in Pakistan, with a focus on grains, vegetables, and fruits. Storage bases will be built in Islamabad and Gwadar in the first phase, then Karachi, Lahore, and another in Gwadar, in the second phase, and between 2026-2030, Karachi, Lahore and Peshawar, will each see another storage base.

In 2015, China imported one hundred sixty billion American dollars' worth of agricultural products.

China can also make most of the Pakistani market, in cheap raw materials, to develop the textiles, and garments industry, and help soak up surplus labour forces in Kashgar, to develop the city, into an industry cluster area, integrating textiles, printing and dyeing, clothing and garment processing.

By 2023, Xinjiang will become the largest cotton textile industry base in China and the most important clothing export base in Western China. The largest city, Urumqi, will turn into the fashion capital of Central Asia.

Fibre optic connectivity between China and Pakistan will prepare the ground for new digital television services, disseminating Chinese culture, and electronic monitoring and control systems, ensuring the security of the project.

The safe city project will deploy explosive detectors, and scanners, to cover major roads, and crowded places in urban areas, to conduct real-time monitoring.

The plan envisages a terrestrial cable across the Khunderjab to Islamabad, and a submarine landing station in Gwadar, linked to Sukkur. From there, the backbone will link the two in Islamabad, as well as all major cities, in Pakistan. Huawei is even installing the Pakistan-East Africa Cable Express, which will connect Gwadar to China's new military base, in Djibouti in 2019.

Hence, under Belt and Road, countries open their policy-making processes to other countries, so that foreign companies could enter.

In Kazakhstan, Chinese companies and the Chinese state have invested in the development of industrial clusters, intended to sell titanium dioxide, silicon dioxide, and vanadium pentoxide to China, for use in aircraft and aerospace industries. Recent industrial projects include Kazakhstan Aluminum, the Kaz Minerals copper mine in Aktogay, and Petrochina's pet coke project, in Pavlodar, all of which are partly funded by Beijing's policy banks, China Development Bank, and Export-Import Bank of China.

These are part of fifty joint Kazakhstan-China industrial capacity cooperation projects, agreed in 2015, worth twenty-five to thirty billion American dollars, over five years, and intended to create industrial cluster cooperation zones, in transport infrastructure, manufacturing, construction and agriculture.

In Belt and Road, capital ought to be used in ways, that further, China's industrial transformation, and should not be squandered.

In Malaysia, China is building Forest City, a hundred billion joint venture, between China's giant home building company, Country Garden, from Guandong Province, and the Sultan of Johor.

Interestingly, Eurasian Resources Group, a Kazakh company, has partnered with China Non-Ferrous Metals Group, Export-Import Bank of China, Industrial and Commercial Bank of China, and China Export and Credit Insurance Corporation, to complete an eight hundred million copper and cobalt project in the Democratic Republic of Congo's Katanga district. The project, which was given a green signal in 2018, to supply China with two hundred thousand tons of cobalt, its single biggest supplier, enough to make batteries for five hundred thousand electric vehicles.

Kazakhstan's 'bright path', 'hundred concrete steps', and 'strategy 2050' industrial policies have been planned to intersect with China's industrial plans, since the outset of Belt and Road in 2013.

***

The best image of the Belt and Road is not trains crossing the Eurasian super continent, or the ports and industrial parks, opening along the way. It is about cities being built from the scratch.

These are the things that will change the physical, and human landscape of the world, creating new standards of life, new ideas, and newer adventures.

It is not about the territory; the economy is what matters. Nor it is about which country has the biggest companies, which can be relocated or disrupted. It is about ecosystems, the collection of companies, workers, consumers, the clusters of culture, social life, and economic activity.
But there have been plausible and most common criticism from Western commentators, which is that under the Belt

and Road initiative, decision-makers and companies take undue risks, move too fast, and neglect concerns about the sustainability, of investments. Impatience, too, they think, can turn out to be its worst enemy.

The critics think that Belt and Road could bring massive distortions in how capital is allocated, with potentially serious consequences, for all the countries involved.

According to the Institute of International Finance, between the fourth quarter of 2008, and the first quarter of 2018, China's gross debt, exploded from one hundred seventy-one per cent, to two hundred ninety-nine per cent of the GDP.

In recent times, China has started to tighten the reins on debt, with debt growing slowing to the lowest rate, for more than a decade. Economists comprehend a slowdown in the Chinese economy, but even if risks are well managed, a reduction in credit creation will interfere with the scope and ambition, of many ongoing Belt and Road initiatives.

In June 2018, Financial Times reported that China is scaling back investments in Ethiopia, in the face of growing foreign exchange shortages. Business people, diplomats, and bankers said that the Chinese entities were taking a more cautious approach.

After a new government in Malaysia was formed, it was said that they were reviewing Belt and Road projects in their country, and cancelling most of them to avoid bankruptcy. Myanmar said that it was reviewing the nine billion deep water Kyaukpyu port development, considering it too expensive, and over apprehensions that it could fall under Beijing's control, in case the country defaults on debt.

The amount of debt Myanmar would need to take on for its share of the project would be about two billion American dollars or about three per cent of its GDP. Mahathir Mohammad, who won the 2018 Malaysian elections, complained during the campaign that Forest City showed that Malaysia was giving its most valuable and beautiful land to foreigners, and Chinese projects had no benefit, at large, to Malaysia, as even workers were bought from China.

Therefore, if risks are put onto participant countries, it will ensure that investments become divisive political issues, poisoning relationships, between China and other countries.

In many places in South and Southeast Asia, and elsewhere, China is struggling with accusations of corruption, which become part of the political cycle.

Politicians, who are close to Chinese political stances, are vulnerable to accusations for their campaigns from opposition parties. For example, from Cambodia, to Pakistan, and to Maldives, all of which had elections in 2018, opposition forces are using Chinese-funded projects against the incumbent governments.

Currently, Pakistan has fallen behind on payments for electricity, from new Chinese power projects. The Belt and Road is certainly contributing to the balance and payments crises there.

Raw materials are required to construct buildings, bridges, and roads, and Pakistan must bring all of them from abroad. The same applies to heavy machinery, where Pakistan imports are set to top twenty-seven billion

American dollars. Pakistan can pay for Chinese machinery with Chinese loans, but unfortunately, these loans are due before the economic gains that will be used to pay for them are accrued.

A bailout from International Monetary Fund seems inevitable, but it will create newer difficulties for China Pakistan Economic Corridor, including strict restrictions on borrowing and spending and transparency requirements for existing Chinese loans and projects.

In fact, the Chinese embassy in Pakistan responded to reports, about a connection between the Belt and Road, and the debt crises in Pakistan.

It was argued that forty-two per cent of Pakistan's foreign debt is owed to multilateral financial institutions, with Chinese preferential loans, accounting for only ten per cent of the total. Adding to this complexity, then-United States Secretary of State, Mike Pompeo warned in August, that any potential IMF bailout for Pakistan's new government should not provide funds, to pay off Chinese lenders.

In September 2018, a report by Financial Times suggested that Pakistan might follow Malaysia, in attempting to revise the terms of the Belt and Road initiative. Pakistan's membership of the cabinet responsible for textiles, commerce, industry, and investment, described the project as unfair, insufficiently thought through, and disadvantageous to local companies.

IMF's managing director, Christine Lagarde, in 2018, summed up the concerns when she warned Chinese policymakers, at a conference in Beijing to avoid unneeded and unsustainable projects in participant countries, with heavy debt burdens.

In 2018, Financial Times published an editorial arguing that Belt and Road, was an accident waiting to happen. That is why, it seems that the Chinese thought process, over the initiative, is more political than financial, so that they can control the sources of income and be relatively less strict on the dispensations of credit.

As the Belt and Road initiative gains speed, China is increasingly finding that it cannot provide the required financial resources on its own.

To attempt to fill the Belt and Road initiative from home, using Chinese banks, at a time, when the economy is slowing down, and when the banks are saddled with bad loans, would expose its financial system to various risks.

Hence, it is essential for China to gain access to global financial markets, to complement its domestic resources. World financial hubs, such as Dubai, Singapore, Zurich, or even London, could play a vital role.

China indeed continues to limit access to its financial service market, with cross-border lending, and offshore bond issuance, facing numerous legal and political limitations. Those unfamiliar with the reasons for China's financial protectionism understand that they are less immediately connected to their economic and industrial policy goals, than to their political imperatives. However, the Belt and Road is a high priority for the Chinese government, so it may propel wider discussions about financial market access.

If the question about opening the Chinese financial market is a political one, any country seeking to engage in it needs to address it as such.

There remains an enormous potential to make progress, through dialogue, between public and private stakeholders, and to provide motivation, on both sides.

Belt and Road is meant to provide China with alternatives, reduce its dependency on the world order, and limit risks.

It is very likely, or perhaps inevitable, that the Belt and Road will become more decentralised, or in other words, less Sino-centric, over time, which is not every different from the America-led world order.

Similarly, the Belt and Road may involve a complex system, where companies occupy different levels, in its hierarchy, and some may even acquire managing rights in the initiative.

It is no surprise that debt has emerged as the major challenge faced by the Belt and Road, but for some commentators, it is a part of a grand scheme. According to this view, China deliberately saddles countries with debt, to make them more vulnerable, to its influence. One commentator goes as far as to argue that it is better for China if the projects do not do well because that increases the debt burden for participant countries. Some countries are overwhelmed by debt loads, are forced to sell stakes in critical projects, or hand over their management to Chinese state-owned firms.

Over the second half of 2018, signs of internal discontent with the Belt and Road started to emerge in the public view, a development made more surprising, by the tight control, over public expressions, of doubt over major policy lines. Retired professor of physics, at Shandong University, Sun Wenguang, during a protest, when he was taken away said: 'regular people are poor, let us not throw our money in Africa. Throwing money around like this does not do any good for our country, or our society.'

On 24 July, Xu Zhangrun, a law professor at Tsinghua University, published a lengthy online critique of China's present political and social condition.

He called Belt and Road, to be a form of 'excessive political aid.' For a developing country, with a large population, many of whom live in pre-modern poverty, such behaviour is uncalled for, Xu argues, stressing that average Chinese are most frequently offended.

According to his perspective, the state scatters large sums of money through international aid, to little, or no benefit. For Xu, the internationalism of the Belt and Road is no more than a form of vanity politics, or flashy showmanship.

***

CHINA BOOM IN SOUTH AND CENTRAL AMERICA

It was at the end of 19th century, the Panama railroad company imported thousands of Chinese workers to lay the tracks for railway lines that would later lead to the construction of the Panama Canal. They settled in Panama afterwards, and live in the enclaves known as the neighbourhoods of Chino-Panamenos, or Chinese Panamanians.

They came to the Americas, as labourers, on large infrastructural projects. However, many decades later, they are now coming to the Americas, not as labourers, on such projects, they are now the bankers that are financing them.

To name a few, Chinese policy banks and entrepreneurs are pouring billions of dollars into the Twin Ocean Railroad Connection, a five-thousand-kilometre high-speed railway project that will connect Brazil's Atlantic coast, to the Pacific Coast of Peru, and into a controversial new canal through Nicaragua.

These, and many other similar projects, will help get Latin America's soy beans, iron ore, copper, and petroleum to China faster, help China sell its products to Latin America, and gain new trading routes, for both China and Latin America alike.

Latin America experienced a China Boom from 2003 to

2012, until it started to wane off.

During the China Boom, Latin America's economy grew by 3.6 per cent per year, the best surge since the state-led industrialisation period, which stretched from the 1930s to 1982. It would not have come at a better time, when the region's economies experienced slow growth, and financial instability, for over two decades, under the so-called Washington Consensus.

China's Boom has helped to erase various inequalities, in Latin America, and helped many countries, to recover from the global financial crises, of 2008-2009. China filled the gap, when Latin American trade and investment, with Europe and the United States, struggled to recover from the crises.
Currently, Latin America's economic prospects are taking a turn, as China's voracious appetite for Latin American natural resources, has begun to decline, as China balances its economic model from an export-led industry towards more of a consumer-based economy.

At the same time, China's new alliance with Latin America is seen as a major challenge to the United States, a super power that has long considered the Americas as its backyard.

***

China came to the rescue, of many struggling Latin American economies, lately, when Xi Jingping travelled to the region, in 2013, with a big financial package.

It eventually began selling and purchasing into the region, by guzzling oil from Venezuela, Ecuador, and Mexico to fuel its fleet of cars, trucks, and container ships.

China has wired more than half of the world's consumer electronic products with copper from Chile and Peru. Much of the steel in China's new cities is made with iron ore from Brazil.

As standards have risen, the Chinese eat more beef from cattle that are fed with soya beans from Argentina and Brazil. Also, Chinese companies have flocked to the Americas, to invest in these commodities, backed by China's state-run development banks.

At the turn of the twenty-first century, Latin American trade with China was only one per cent, of the total Latin American trade, amounting to only one billion American dollars. By 2013, it fetched around two hundred eighty-nine billion American dollars. China stood as the number one trading partner for many Latin American countries, such as Brazil, Peru, Chile, and others.

China's demand for Latin American commodities had double that impact, it is because China's consumption of those goods, made them scarcer, and the prices of goods went up, in the global market, allowing the region to enjoy a massive commodity boom. The commodity booms triggered investment in the region's commodity sector by Chinese companies and other global firms.

But, the most remarkable thing is that China has provided a massive amount of finance to Latin American governments for infrastructure, mining, and energy projects.

China has provided upward of one hundred nineteen billion American dollars in loans, and lines of credit to Latin American governments, since 2003. It has been a saviour of Latin American governments, in many ways, mainly through the appetite for its commodities, especially in the wake of global financial crises, when trade, and finance from the West dried up.

That is how Latin America enjoyed China's Boom, by growing at an annual rate of 3.6 per cent, from 2003 to 2013. And, it was the first time, when Latin American governments pondered removing rising social inequalities, from their society.

*****

It has been argued by economists that Latin Americans have not capitalised on the China Boom in many ways.

As the infamous 'resource curse' predicts, during the commodity boom, money pours into the commodity sector. Commodity booms, thus, create windfalls for the commodity sector, but fewer jobs. It causes exchange rate appreciation of the currencies, making non-commodity exports, more expensive.

As money poured in, commodity producers got rich, and non-commodity exports became less competitive. What eventually happened was that seventy-eight per cent of Latin American manufacturing was under threat from their Chinese counterparts, in world markets, during the boom.

The infrastructure, energy, and mining projects, that were the source of so much investment, from the Chinese, became endemic to environmental degradation, and social conflict in Latin America.

According to World Bank estimates, the economic costs of environmental degradation, during the China Boom, were an annual 8.6 per cent of GDP. As Chinese companies flocked into the region, they deforested the Amazon, polluted waterways, and sometimes mistreated the indigenous and local communities, while the governments turned a blind eye.

According to IMF, Latin Americans saved less from the China Boom than in past ones, and United Nations calculations show that the government's fiscal revenue did not increase in proportion, to the windfall. Thus, it was no surprise that the investment in the region was so low, overall.

The lack of investment in long-run growth and sustainable development will affect the economies of the region. At this point, it also remains unclear whether Latin American manufacturing exports will be competitive enough, to seize the opportunity, to meet Chinese demand, for such products.

***

It was in January 2015, when the Chinese pondered on the Latin American region, and put together a cooperation plan with the region, aiming for reform.

China pledged to boost trade to five hundred billion American dollars, and investment to two hundred fifty American dollars, over the next decade. China also created a new set of funds of around thirty-five billion American dollars, for infrastructure investment in Latin America.

However, Chinese funding also comes with a few strings attached. China might demand that Chinese companies have a hand in some projects, but has avoided meddling in domestic policy. The new cooperation plan also puts a premium on cooperation in science, technology, and innovation policy.

China pledges to start a dialogue about the establishment of Chinese industrial parks, across Latin America. If Latin America puts in place the proper reforms that enable such zones to benefit the broader economy, China's industrial parks can help diversify Latin American economies, and make them more competitive.

Latin American exchange rates will be depreciating relative to China's Boom peaks as well. That will make the prices of Latin American exports more affordable across the world, and their industries more competitive. New industrial opportunities, competitive exchange rates, and increasing demand for consumer goods in China can be harnessed into diversified growth for Latin America.

China's cooperation plan for Latin America also boasts a built-in dialogue on environmental cooperation. Recognising the environmental and social impacts of its trade and investment with the region, this can be a forum to enable China's firms and financial institutions to upgrade their social and environmental safeguards.

Such an outcome will not only benefit people and the environment across the Americas but will also help China's bottom line. Environmental and social conflict in the Americas can trigger costly delays, and shutdowns that cut into profits, and the image of China's vision for South-South cooperation. China's economic relationship with Latin America remains that is based on natural resource-based commodities.

China has been looking to regain its place at the top of the world economy, while Latin America has been searching for an economic path, that will help the region catch up to the rest of the world.

***

Between 2008 and 2012, 86.4 per cent of Latin American exports that went to China (over 15 per cent of total exports from the region) were in the primary commodities sectors, and 13.3 per cent in manufacturing.

Iron ore tops the list, and Brazil is China's main trading partner. China gets one-third of all its imported iron ore from Latin America, and almost all of it from Brazil. In 2012, China imported six hundred million tons of iron ore, and one-third of that came from Brazil.

Over the years, as the Chinese economy boomed, so did its demand for soy. During China Boom, both soy seeds, and oils were Latin America's second-largest export to China. Brazil is the region's largest exporter of beans to China, and Argentina is the largest exporter of oils. Colombia, Bolivia, and Paraguay export soy to China as well.

In 2009, five eight per cent of all Chinese imports of soybeans came from Latin America, mostly from Brazil. In that same year, ninety-five per cent of China's imports of soy oil came from Argentina, representing seventy-three per cent of the country's oil exports.

Copper is Latin America's third largest export to China. Like the steel made from iron ore in Brazil, copper from Chile, and Peru is often a building material found in China's new cities and factory buildings.

Copper is also a source of a key transmitter of electricity, and copper from Chile and Peru laces the wires of parts and components in China's vast, and growing electronics, telecommunications, and auto industries.

Fifty-four per cent of China's copper imports come from Chile and Peru. Copper also has another use that is unique to China. It is used as collateral for credit, or a hedging device. Usually, an importer in China places the value of copper purchase, as a deposit in a bank, in exchange for a line of credit for the same amount.

The importer then resells the copper in China and uses the proceeds to invest (or speculate) on other asset classes, such as real estate. In other cases, copper importers in China purchase copper and store it in a warehouse, as collateral, for a loan, from a foreign bank.

Venezuela, Colombia, Brazil and Ecuador, and Mexico together provide Latin America's fourth largest export to China – petroleum. In 2013, China consumed 10.7 million barrels of oil per day but produced less than half of the amount. In 2014, China became the largest importer of oil in the world, although more than half of the oil came from the Middle East, and around ten per cent came from the Americas, with Venezuela, and Brazil, being the largest providers.

South America's vast deposits of energy, raw materials, and food are uniquely suited for China's growing demand. Mexico, and Central America, however, have fared less well, in the China lottery, and have not experienced as much of a China Boom.

Mexico and Costa Rica have been exporting significant and growing amounts of radios, televisions, and integrated circuits, for computers to China. Yet these exports are relatively small, and those countries have significant trade deficits with China.

There is also more to trade than just exports. Imports from China have been just as remarkable, as exports to China for Latin America. Whereas Latin Americans ship out primary commodities, they import a wide variety of manufactured goods from China.

Increasingly, office equipment, electronics, batteries, clothing, and appliances come from China to the Americas.

***

Chinese presence in Latin America is no longer only through export and import markets.

Many Chinese companies have set up shops in Latin America now. China's oil and gas companies can be found wherever gas and oil reserves are found in Latin America – Argentina, and Brazil. Colombia, Ecuador, Peru. Chinese mining companies have scattered down the coast of Peru and then East into Bolivia. Chinese manufacturers are also now based in Latin America.

Anyone who purchased Lenovo Think Pad will have likely purchased it from Lenovo plants in Mexico and Brazil. Chinese auto companies use Uruguay and Mexico as export platforms, to the large MERCOSUR and NAFTA markets nearby.

In 2000, Latin America hardly registered Chinese investment, by 2012, China was the third largest investor in Latin America, just behind the United States and the Netherlands.

In 2012, Chinese firms poured 9.2 billion American

dollars into Latin American countries, in the form of new plants, mergers or acquisitions.

The stock of Chinese foreign direct investment in Latin America by 2012 was approximately fifty billion American dollars. Interestingly, the pattern of investment largely tracks the pattern of trade, with over ninety-four per cent of all Chinese FDI into Latin America going into the energy, mining, and food sectors.

What also makes Chinese investments in Latin America distinct is that it is dominated by state-owned enterprises, rather than private-sector multinationals.

According to calculations, by Enrique Dussel Peters, economist, and director of the Centre for China-Mexico Studies at the National Autonomous University of Mexico, eighty-seven per cent of all Chinese foreign investment in Latin America is from state-owned companies, and ninety-nine per cent of all state-owned company investments in Latin America were concentrated in the energy and raw materials sector.

Private sector actors represent just thirteen per cent of the total and concentrate largely in the manufacturing and service sectors. These private sector firms are largely not financed by the CDB and CHEXIM, with exception of firms, such as Huawei and Geely. Rather, private sector firms are financing their globalisation through retained earnings.

By far, the largest Chinese investments in Latin America are in the energy and mining sectors.

With just a few exceptions, these investments are dominated by China's big three state-owned firms

– China National Petroleum Corporation (CNPC), China National Offshore Oil Corporation (CNOOC), and the China Petroleum and Chemical Corporation (SINOPEC), which are backed by finance from the CDB, their in-house financing units, and the larger government apparatus, enabling China is go out policy.

And, China's overseas oil and gas companies are more likely to sell a newly acquired barrel of oil, on world markets, than ship it at home.

Argentina and Brazil are the recipients of most Chinese investments, in the oil and gas sectors, though Colombia, Ecuador, Peru, and Venezuela are also destinations for Chinese firms. The two largest acquisitions in Argentina are by the Chinese firms CNOOC and SINOPEC.

In March 2010, CNOOC acquired a fifty per cent stake in the Argentine firm, Bridas Company, for a staggering $3.1 billion.

CNOOC teamed with Bridas to mix its knowledge of offshore and onshore production, leaving the company to be largely managed by the founders of Bridas, the Bulgheroni family.

Since Bridas has a forty per cent stake in Pan American Energy (PAE) Corporation, the merger granted CNOOC access to Argentina's large Cerro Dragon petroleum reserve, operated by PAE. PAE's exports in 2011 were $4.6 billion.

Also, in 2010, SINOPEC acquired twenty-three fields in Santa Cruz, Chubut, and Mendoza, Argentina. SINOPEC's exports from Argentina in 2012 were $1.2 billion.

SINOPEC's largest acquisition in Latin America was the purchase of a 40 per cent stake in the Spanish firm Repsol's Brazilian operations for $7.1 billion. SINOPEC reportedly invested an additional $1 billion into the firm's operations in 2013.

Related to Chinese investments in the electricity sector, State Grid Corporation, the largest electricity company in the world, did the acquisition of seven national electricity transmission companies, and twelve transmission lines, making State Grid Corporation the fourth largest energy transmission company in Brazil.

Mining investments are also of an immense scale. The largest merger and acquisition (M&A) project in the mining sector was in 2011, when a group of five Chinese state-owned enterprises purchased a fifteen per cent stake in the Brazilian mining firm *Companhia Brasileira de Metalurgie e Mineracao* for two billion American dollars, granting the Chinese firm access to rare earth elements in Brazil. However, the country, where Chinese firms are most active is Peru.

Chinese mining firms are engaged in at least eight major mining projects in that country, including the Shougang iron mine, where copper deposits date back to 1992.

The Aluminium Corporation of China (CHINALCO) acquired the Canadian firm Peru Copper and has invested more than three billion American dollars into its new Peruvian copper operations to date. The project is named for Mount Toromocho (in Spanish: 'no bulls no horns'), the site for the copper mine, which will result in hollowing out an open pit larger than New York City's Central Park.

China has been promoting investment in Latin America's

agricultural sector as well, especially in the planting of oil seeds, cotton, and vegetables, the harvesting and shipping of timber, and ocean fisheries. China's Ministry of Commerce created a special fund for Chinese agricultural companies, to go out in these sectors. According to detailed research by Margaret Myers of Washington-based Inter-American Dialogue, in 2005, the Pengxin Group, a private Chinese company, purchased land for soybean production in Santa Cruz, Bolivia. Chinese firms Zhenjiang Fudi and Chongqing Grain Group form part of similar purchases in Brazil. Chinese companies are also getting in on Chile's world-class wineries, with the Chinese wine firm Great Wall purchasing Chilean land for such purposes.

Myers also documents that Chinese agricultural processing firms such as Chongqing Grain Group, Sanhe Hopefull, and China National Heavy Machinery Corporation have been investing in pressing plants, mills, and more across the Americas.

In Caixin, a Chinese media source, Myers attributes China's agricultural expansion into Latin America as being a result of a 'two markets, two resources' approach to food security, wherein the country works to improve domestic production capacity in staple foods, while seeking to control production, processing, and logistics, for commodities like soy, that cannot be supplied domestically in sufficient quantities.

However, compared to energy and mining, or even manufacturing, Chinese investments in agriculture in Latin America is very small.

There is a growing presence of China's investment in Latin America's manufacturing as well. Its investment is mainly to better serve itself, as an export platform to nearby markets, and to acquire technology and knowledge.

Lenovo started in Brazil in 2005, shortly after acquiring the Think Pad. In 2012, Lenovo acquired Brazil's CCE and doubled its market share in Brazil. In 2009, Lenovo opened a manufacturing and distribution plant in an industrial cluster of Monterrey, Mexico, where it produces and sells its products to three NAFTA countries.

China's car companies are also going global and can be found in Brazil, Mexico, and Uruguay. Between 2006, to 2012, China announced a total of nearly six billion dollars of auto-related investments in Latin America.

Uruguay is becoming a hot spot and a testing ground for China's fast-growing automotive companies, too. It is also a popular place to manufacture goods for re-export into other MERCOSUR countries. It receives the third largest foreign direct investments in Latin America, as compared to Chile and Panama. China has awakened this trend, with textiles, telecom, chemicals, and auto companies, flocking to Uruguay.

China also has stakes in Latin America's telecom and banking sectors. One of China's big four banks, ICBC, took an eighty per cent stake in Standard Bank of Argentina, in 2011, for seven hundred million American dollars.

As per the research done by Evan Ellis, one of the closet watchers of China in Latin America, ICBC now operates ninety-nine branches with over one million clients and three thousand two hundred employees in Argentina. The other four banks are increasing their presence in Latin America as well, with CCB and BOC, establishing a presence in Brazil, and CCB in Peru.

Also, Chinese demand for Latin American primary

commodities could not have come at a better time. The region was plagued with a half-decade of financial crises, and Chinese demand was a big lift.

As China was demanding so much iron ore, copper, soy, and other commodities, these commodities became scarcer. As the laws of supply and demand dictate, scarcity brings higher prices. Hence, the commodity super cycle spurred China's rise and was associated with one of the largest and longest commodity price spikes in modern history.

Between 2003 and 2011, China accounted for fifty per cent of the growth in key commodities that Latin America provides to markets. After the financial crisis, China accounted for around eighty-three per cent of the growth.

So, not only did Latin American countries do better by selling to China, they got higher prices when they sold their commodities the world over. The result was higher export earning for Latin America. Between 2002 to 2007, it was between forty-one billion American dollars to seventy-three billion American dollars.

The increasing terms of trade for Latin America helped the region accumulate more foreign exchange reserves, which helped boost investor confidence, and provide insurance in case of pressure on their exchange rates, increasing export revenue, which can also bring more tax revenue, and reduce pressure on public budgets.

Indeed, it was by the mid-2000s, the Latin American economies started to become interlinked with the fate of the Chinese economy. The increase in the growth of the Chinese economy resulted in growth in Latin America. During Latin America's China Boom, from 2003 to 2013, the region grew at 3.6 per cent per year, and 2.4 per cent in per capita terms. That puts the China Boom, the largest per capita growth rate in over a hundred years, though in terms of absolute growth.

One area where Latin American nations did leverage China's gift was by setting up programs that reduced poverty and equality. During China Boom, social inequality reduced, as much as it did during the Washington Consensus. According to noted Latin American economist, Nora Lustig, the leading reason for inequality reduction was an increase in worker incomes. The other reasons were skill level rises, and the developing world is called conditional cash transfers, or CCTs. Under a CCT, households are given funds on the condition that they send their children to school and get regular checkups.

***

Xi Jinping, like his predecessor, Hu Jintao, visited Latin America and provided upward of $5.3 billion in financing for energy and infrastructure projects. At the same time, Chinese businessmen started negotiations with Daniel Ortega of Nicaragua to build and finance an alternative to the Panama Canal through that country.

Since 2001, Chinese heads of state have made just as many visits to Latin American countries, as the United States has, but have left upward of $119 billion in loans of credit behind in the process.

Dollar diplomacy, the William Taft era policy of providing finance to Latin American governments to promote US Commerce, and political interests, has been replaced by 'Yuan Diplomacy.'

By 2014, Chinese development banks were providing more finance to Latin American governments than the World Bank, or the Inter-American Bank (IDB). In 2010, and 2014, China provided Latin American governments with more funds than the World Bank, the Inter-American Development Bank, and the US Export-Import Bank combined.

By nature, Chinese finance tends to flow to countries that have a hard time gaining access to global capital markets. The largest recipients of Chinese finance are Argentina, Brazil, Ecuador, and Venezuela.

China has also begun to finance Mexico to get in on the ground floor, of new oil explorations, while more timid Western financial markets watch with more caution.

China's billions in finance are more in line with what Latin American nations want, rather than what Western development experts say they need.

Whereas the US and International Financial Institutions (IFIs) such as World Bank, and IMF tend to finance in line with trade liberalisation, health and education, Chinese loans tend to go into energy, infrastructure, and industry projects, in a region, that has an infrastructure gap of two hundred sixty billion American dollars per year.

As of now, Latin America's roads, ports, telecommunications networks, and energy systems are severely lacking.

Chinese loans do not come with harsh strings attached, as in the case with IFI finance. China has become bold and has taken on more risk, in part, because of its innovative finance schemes. Half of the Chinese finance is in the form of the unique lending instrument – the commodity-backed loan, where Latin American countries ship hundreds and thousands of barrels of oil, to China, to repay their loans.

Not only has the new financing helped Latin American governments meet their needs, but it has also improved the profile of Latin Americans in the eyes of the global investment community.

For example, the rating giant, Moody's upgraded the country's bond rating on two occasions, when Ecuador continuously paid back paid China in oil and dollars. In other words, China helped Ecuador secure access to global markets. That is the reason, why many polls cite that China has a more positive influence in Latin American, in comparison, with the United States.

Also, at the turn of the century, the only banks in Latin American nations were the World Bank and the Inter-American Development Bank. Now there was a new bank called the China Development Bank in a town.

Between 2005, to 2014, China's policy banks provided up to one hundred nineteen billion American dollars to fifteen Latin American governments, with an average-sized loan of approximately $1.7 billion.

Latin American share of China's global policy bank lending is likely the largest of all such lending by China. For 2009-2010, Chinese finance in Latin America was around forty-seven billion American dollars. Between 2003 to 2011, China provided eighty billion American dollars to Latin America.

Most of the China's finance to Latin American governments is in the form of bilateral lines of credit or loans at commercial rates. In 2007, China and Venezuela set up the China-Venezuela Joint Fund (Fondo Conjunto Chino Venezolano, FCCV). The FCCV is financed jointly with Venezuelan National Development Fund (Fonden). The FCCV is managed by the Venezuelan Economic and Social Development Bank (Bandes) and is designed to finance infrastructure projects in Venezuela. In 2013, China and IDB established a two billion China Cofinancing Fund for Latin America and the Caribbean.

Chinese and other big development banks, do no overlap significantly in Latin America, because they give different size loans, to different sectors, in different countries. Not only is the scale of Chinese finance different in Latin America, but so is the form of finance. Most of the Chinese finance in the region goes into large infrastructure projects, energy, and mining projects. The Chinese banks channel eighty-seven per cent of their loans into the energy, mining, and infrastructure sectors.

China started providing Latin American governments with aid, as early as 1996, when it granted three hundred eighty-seven million American dollars to the region, and has now provided aid to eighteen countries in the region.

In Haiti, China provided aid as well, by sending in rescue and search teams, and helped with medicine, shelter, food, and water. Other examples include emergency aid, for the dengue fever epidemic in Ecuador, and to recover from mudslides in Bolivia, a hurricane in Uruguay, an earthquake in Peru, and a flu epidemic in Mexico.

And, about half of Latin America's contracts, with Chinese policy banks are commodity-backed. All of China's commodity-backed loans to Latin America are secured in oil. Most of these loans for oil deals go to Venezuela, and Ecuador, and one to Brazil. Venezuela and Ecuador, each, have a very difficult time borrowing in conventional capital markets. In Venezuela's case, it is due to economic and political uncertainty, and in Ecuador, it is due to the 2008 default.

Hence, China's policy banks are willing to take on more risks, for these countries, and projects, by securing the finance with oil. In general, the loans for oil deals in Latin America entail a package put together by CDB, the debtor nation's Ministry of Finance, the national oil company exporting the oil, and the Chinese company that will be importing the oil.

The Latin American Ministry of finance signs the loan agreement with CDB, and the Chinese importer signs a purchase agreement, with the national oil company, that is specified in barrels of oil per day.

The proceeds are deposited into an escrow account at the CDB until the loan is repaid.

It is thus not the export of oil that repays the loan, but the proceeds from the sale of the oil on spot market prices on the day of sale. CDB grants a billion-dollar loan to the oil-exporting government like that of Ecuador.

Ecuador's state oil company, Petro Ecuador, signs a contract to sell Chinese oil companies hundreds and thousands of barrels of oil per day, until the loan has been paid back, perhaps for ten years. Chinese oil companies purchase the oil at market prices and deposit their payments into Petro Ecuador's CDB bank account. CDB withdraws the interest payments and principal repayment, a pre-agreed amount that might reach thirty per cent of the total oil revenue, directly from Petro Ecuador's account.

The rest of the revenue returns to Ecuador. A four-billion-dollar loan to Venezuela was secured in 2011 with sales of two hundred thirty thousand barrels per day. Ecuador received a one-billion-dollar line of credit from China, in 2009, that is partially secured with thirty-nine thousand barrels of oil per day. Two Chinese loans to Latin America are supplier's credits from Petro China to Petro Ecuador.

PetroChina is part of the large Chinese state-owned oil company Chinese National Petroleum Corporation.

Except for some lines of credit, to Venezuela, which is co-financed with Venezuela that goes into infrastructural projects, the bulk of commodity-backed Chinese finance to these countries is for oil exploration and extraction.

Chinese loans often come with a tacit understanding that Chinese companies will be doing a significant amount of the work related to the project, or that the project will involve Chinese imports. In China, these credits have been called different names: *'hu hui dai kuan'* (mutual benefit loan) and *'shiyou, xindai gongcheng yi lanzi hezuo xiangmu'* (cooperation package of oil, credit, construction projects).

In a three hundred forty million American dollar loan to Jamaica for infrastructure, in 2010, sixty per cent went to a Chinese firm to do harbour construction, and forty per cent to local firms.

CDB's 2010 one billion American dollar loan for oil to Ecuador mandated twenty per cent Chinese purchases. At the other extreme, CHEXIM gives hundred per cent export credits, like a 2010 $1.7 billion loan to pay a Chinese company to build a Coca-Cola Sinclair hydroelectric dam in Ecuador. In a 2011 loan to Ecuador to finance

Ecuador's annual budget, and to invest in hydroelectric energy projects, the hydro projects were awarded to Chinese firms.

Since Venezuela committed to spending the majority of its 2010 twenty billion American dollar loan on Chinese goods, and services, CDB denominated half in Chinese *yuan*.

Though this is the largest Chinese currency loan to date, CHEXIM has also issued *yuan*-denominated lines of credit, to Jamaica, and Bolivia for equipment and construction.

Whether the loans are issued in dollars, *yuan*, or simply establish a line of credit with a given Chinese company, the purchase requirements allow Chinese banks to reduce their exposure to default risk.

The various innovative financing methods help China to fulfil their multiple objectives, on both ends of the transaction. They help China establish diverse, long-term oil supply chains, promote Chinese exports, and put dollar reserves to more productive use than the low-interest rate.

***

Chinese finance in Latin America is also becoming popular, in the region, because it operates under a different set of enforcement standards when compared to conventional finance.

China's policy banks are more apt to invest in these countries, because of their innovative finance schemes, and the strategic need for resources, that such countries offer to China.

When Chinese banks do come, they do not impose policy conditionalities of any kind, in keeping with the general foreign policy of non-intervention. That is the reason, why Latin American banks have formed coalitions against the IMF and the World Bank, in recent years.

Hugo Chavez once declared that the Chinese differ from other multilateral loans because it comes without strings attached.

To prevent Venezuela's from defaulting, China stepped in. The country, first under Hugo Chavez, and then under Nicolas Maduro, were able to fund public expenditures, given the high price of oil, in the 2000s, and due to a joint fund with China. Without these sources, Venezuela would have had a very tough time dealing with the international capital markets.

According to official reports, Venezuela was able to renegotiate some of the details of their 'loans for oil' with China, to meet anticipated cash flow problems in 2014.

One of Venezuela's loans for oil required a minimum shipment of three hundred thousand barrels of oil per day, to make sure that the loan would be paid back, at a rate between forty to seventy American dollars per barrel. As prices soared too high to over a hundred American dollars, Venezuela was overpaying for its loans, and the Chinese were reimbursing China for those windfalls.

The new arrangement allows Venezuela to only sell enough oil, as is necessary for the loan, avoid delayed reimbursements, and extend the three-year repayment period deadline later. The price of oil continued to plummet, as did the value of the country's currency. Apparently, with Chinese approval, Venezuela moved four billion American dollars in loans from China that were set aside as infrastructure and development loans, into their foreign exchange reserves account.

When Ecuador defaulted many of its debts, in 2008, and has been shunned, from conventional capital markets, the CDB and CHEXIM, also stepped in, with ten billion American dollar loans, and lines of credit to Ecuador.

Some of these loans have been for discretionary budget spending for Ecuador.

China has also thrown a lifeline to Argentina. In 2013, the central banks of China and Argentina agreed to an eleven billion American dollar currency swap, over three years. By 2015, Argentina drew on the swap, and converted over one billion American dollars, from *yuan* to dollars, to bolster its foreign reserves as well.

Latin America's most stable economy, from a macroeconomic perspective, Chile, signed a three-year currency deal, with China, in 2015, for $3.6 billion.

In January 2015, China hosted the first-ever China-CELAC cooperation summit. At that venue, China committed twenty billion American dollars in special loans, for Latin American infrastructure cooperation, ten billion American dollars in preferential loans for Latin American countries, and founded a fifty million American dollar China-CELAC Cooperation Fund – this on top of fifty million China-America fund for agricultural research, and development centres, and a five-hundred-thousand-ton food reserve.

It seems that every time a Chinese leader goes to Latin America, he puts his money, where his mouth is. In mid-

2015- Chinese premier Li Keqiang spent just over a week in South America, visiting Brazil, Peru, Colombia, and Chile.

That was long enough to provide ten billion American dollars to Brazil's embattled state-owned oil company Petrobas, facilitate a twenty-seven billion American dollar fund for infrastructure development in Brazil, and a thirty billion American dollar China–Latin America cooperation fund for promoting infrastructure and industrial capacity.

Indeed, China has adapted new financing techniques, to take on more risk, to go where the West could not. This new trade, investment, and finance that surged due to China's rise from 2003 to 2013, in Latin America, can be seen as nothing less than the region's China's boom.

***

According to El Tiempo newspaper, Chinese businessmen descended on the indigenous area of San Andres de Sotavento, and began watching how *Vueltiao*, cowboy-like hats were made.

Shortly after, Chinese versions of *Vueltiao* began to appear in Cartagena. The Chinese version was synthetic and mass-produced, but similar enough in appearance to an authentic *Vueltiao*, that it easily fooled tourists, looking to bring back home, a symbol of Colombia, especially since the Chinese knockoffs sold half the price.

The *Zena* artisans were walloped by the entrance of China into the domestic *Vueltiao* market.

According to Eder Suarez, a local vendor, at their high

point in 2013, the Chinese hats sold more than three times the rate of Colombian hats; in a typical month, Suarez sold one hundred eighty Chinese copies and only sixty authentic hats. While a Chinese hat sells for twenty thousand Colombian Pesos, the cheapest authentic *Vueltiao* sell for forty thousand Pesos.

The Colombia government was quick to act, when people in the Colombian town of Tuchin, called on then President Juan Manuel Santos to act, to defend their cultural symbol, and source of income.

By that time, the government was quick to act. The *Vueltiao* had been marked as 'intellectual property' in 2011, and in 2013, when the Colombian press began to cover the sales of Chinese *Vueltiaos,* the government ordered the suspension of 'production, commercialisation, or sale of all hats, that try to imitate or replicate the hats protected as '*Tejeduria Zenu*', or the hats protected by the '*Sombrero Vueltiao*' brand, to substitute it.

What happened with the Colombian Vueltiao is a symbolic trend that became associated with the China Boom across the Americas. Argentina, and Brazil, lost toys and shoes, and Mexico and Guatemala lost their shirts and computer exports. What China Boom was doing was that it was appreciating the national currencies, and at the same time, there was a subsequent reduction in the competitiveness of manufacturing and other non-commodity export sectors in Latin America.

***

China's trade and investment in Latin America have been a key driver of economic activity, since the turn of the century, but are also partly responsible for the environmental conflict and social conflict in the Americas. Eighty-seven per cent of Latin American exports to China are in mining or agriculture. It should come as no surprise, then, that the environmental impact of Latin America's trade and investment with China is more harmful than economic activity, in the region, that is no directly linked to China.

Each dollar of economic activity in Latin America generates about 1.1 kilograms of carbon pollution.

Latin American exports are more carbon-intensive, given the region's reliance, on natural resources and primary commodities, associated with the clearing of forests and methane emissions.

The carbon intensity of Latin American exports was 1.7 kilograms per dollar. Latin America's China trade is more carbon intensive, nearly two kilograms per dollar.

China trade is much more interested in natural resource-based sectors than the rest of Latin America's trade. Because China-Latin America trade is the fastest-growing area of export activity for Latin America, the implications for climate change are considerable.

Contemporary Chinese investment in Latin America dates to 1992, when one of China's oldest state-owned companies, Shougang purchased the Marcona iron mine in Peru.

Shougang has seemingly fulfilled the worst expectations of Chinese companies.

It was less apt to comply with local environmental regulations, complying only seventy-two per cent of the time, relative to some Swiss, and US firms, which complied eighty-six to ninety per cent of the time.

When audited on its environmental behaviour, Shougang also fired union and indigenous workers, who had a long history of striking for better wages and living conditions, and replaced these workers with Chinese miners.

However, according to recent research, Shougang has made significant improvement and now performs on par with most local and other foreign firms, in terms of safety, environment and labour standards. As a sign that the company is willing and able to adapt to Peruvian and global norms. In 2014, Shougang even agreed to participate in the Extractive Industries Transparency Initiative (EITI).

In the case of China-Latin America investment, the environmental standards of the foreign investor (China) are lower than the standards of the host countries. Hence, there are numerous mistakes on the part of the Chinese side, as their firms struggle to comply with standards abroad that are more stringent than at home.

However, some Chinese firms are showing the willingness and ability to outperform even Swiss and American firms in terms of social responsibility.

The Association of Chinese Enterprises in Peru was formed in 2011 and comprises more than half of the one hundred Chinese firms operating in the country, where the group meets to share the best practices that are put in place.

After the copper giant Aluminum Corporation of China (known as CHINALCO), was ordered to temporarily halt production, when government inspectors found that acidic wastes were seeping into the nearby lakes, the association went to the Peruvian government seeking workshops, on Peruvian environmental regulation.

When Toromocho project was financed by CHINALCO, at three billion American dollars, one of the largest in the world, it pledged to establish itself as meeting or beating global standards, for social and environmental responsibility. For that, the firm has promised to deploy innovative construction technology, and the state-of-the-art acid treatment plant, and responsibly relocate approximately five thousand people.

Each family that moves to New Morococha has been offered their own home, (and title), running water, and a modern sewage system, all paid for by CHINALCO.

The firm also offers higher wages than its competitors and has entered a government-sponsored 'mesa' or roundtable that brings together the numerous stakeholders, in the project (the firm, communities, civil society groups, the government etc.) to navigate the issues.

Another positive development is that Shougang, China Minmetals (another copper firm operating in Peru, as Lumina copper), and oil giant CNPC have now agreed to participate in the EITI in Peru.

The EITI is a cluster of governments, extractive companies, and civil society groups, looking to increase transparency and accountability in the global mining sector.
When a country or firm joins EITI, they are committed to adhering to global standards, reporting taxes, and royalties, to make more transparent their contributions, to the host economy.

As per Sanborn and Chong, Chinese firms were slower to participate, because they needed to get the okay from their corporate headquarters back in China. In 2012, Lumina Copper, another Chinese firm in Peru, was first to enter EITI, Shougang and CNPC followed in 2014.

China's SINOPEC is part of an innovative experiment, in inshore oil drilling that aims to have minimum environmental and social impact. In Ecuador's Amazon Block 16, the Spanish firm Repsol, and its junior partner (with a twenty per cent stake), SINOPEC are experimenting with a new method of oil development, in ecological and socially sensitive areas – termed 'offshore inland' development.

The basic idea of offshore inland development is to create islands in the jungle, where oil companies have as little footprint as possible.

The most central element is not building new roads, to the drilling and exploration sites, but rather helicoptering in key supplies, as if the site is an offshore platform.

The Camisea project in Peru is the first of its kind, has been operating for ten years, and produces over ninety per cent of Peru's natural gas. Equipment comes to the site through barges.

SINOPEC's subsidiary in Ecuador, Tiptop Energy bought a twenty percent stake in the project from Repsol, and has been partaking in and learning from the project. It will be essential for SINOPEC to bring this knowledge and experience, to the new concessions in the Amazon located near the Sapara people.

When governments and civil society organisations have

pursued Chinese companies, the Chinese have agreed to move the location of the entire project, or decided against a project altogether.

The Chinese metallurgy company Jungie, was awarded concessions in Bolivia, for a metal processing plant, and tailings dam, in the municipality of Tacobamba, just north of Potosi. The people of Tacobamba rejected the Jungie proposal, expressing their concerns over the potential impacts of sulphur, and other pollutants, that might result from the project. Jungie worked with the Bolivian government, and the project was relocated to the municipality of Villa de Yocalla, a less remote area, where the local community voted in favour of the project.

Perhaps the most difficult and honourable move, by a Chinese firm, concerning the environment, was the complete withdrawal of China's largest hydroelectric company, Sinohydro, from the Agua, Zarca dam project in Honduras.

Indigenous peoples and environmental advocates claimed that they were not consulted adequately before the project commenced in 2011. The project was wholly rejected in an assembly held by the major of the local community there. Nevertheless, the Honduran government, supplied military forces, to protect the project, and the military reportedly shot and killed the local indigenous leader there. Citing the project as 'unpredictable and uncontrollable,' Sinohydro has wiped its hand cleanly off this project, entirely.

The Chinese company faces stiff resistance from a coalition of global environmental campaigners. The Chinese company has won a concession to build a dam, on Hondura's Patuca River, which may impact the ecological integrity, and indigenous communities around the Rio Platano World Heritage Site – already seen as a threatened tropical rainforest biosphere, that has been placed on UNESCO's endangered list, because of illegal logging and poaching.

***

China has been upgrading and setting guidelines for overseas operations, since 2007, when China's State Forestry Administration put in place the 'Guide on Sustainable Overseas Silviculture by Chinese Enterprises.'

The guidelines require the preservation of high-value forests, and endangered species, as well as consultations with local communities before investments occur.

In 2008, China enacted the 'Guidelines for Environmental and Social Impact Assessments of the China Export and Import Loan Projects'.

In 2013, China's Ministry of Foreign Commerce, along with the Ministry of Environmental Protection (MEP), issued 'Guidelines on Environmental Protection for Overseas Investment and Cooperation' that require environmental impact assessments and work with local communities.

Perhaps, the most interesting is the 2012 'Green Credit Guidelines', created by the China Banking and Regulatory Commission, the Peoples bank of China (PBOC), and the Ministry of Environmental Protection. The guidelines require all bank finance in China – public or private – to adhere to a set of environmental and social norms. However, it is not China's job to be the overarching manager of natural resources and social inclusion in the

Americas. Latin American nations, themselves, need to develop strong, stable, and predictable policies that ensure natural resources are managed wisely.

It is because, in the recent past, the entire policy framework, in Latin America is to promote, as much short-term gain, from economic activity, like natural resource exploitation with accounting, for the social and economic costs, of such activities.

There is evidence that Brazil's famed ruralists, who have been reaping profits from the boom in cattle, and soybean production, since the turn of the century, have been attributed for playing a key role in weakening Brazil's forest code for the Brazilian Amazon. The new code granted amnesty to agricultural landowners, who illegally deforested and allows those landowners, to shrink the amount of forest, they need to protect their lands. From eighty per cent to fifty per cent.

Some estimate that the code change could lead to one hundred ninety million acres worth of deforestation. As China's economy begins to grow, there is pressure to increase the incentive for extraction.

In this context in 2014, the government of Peru passed a law to expedite the approval of extractive projects, which many see as a weakening of environmental and social safeguards for such activity. The law put newer and shorter time limits on project approvals, reducing the amount of time to conduct environmental impact assessments, and to seek community input. It also limits the authority of environmental authorities to update and upgrade environmental assessments, and puts mining industries at key oversight junctures, creating a conflict of interests, while China Boom looms in the background.

In Ecuador, its Citizen Participation Law requires that without the support of most locals, new projects must meet even higher environmental standards.

According to the members of the Sapara nation, majority approval was never sought for the new Andes Petroleum project that is generating so much controversy.

The Ecuadorian government confirms that their government never sought majority community approval, but signed an agreement with the president of the Sapara people, who had been ousted because of the controversy surrounding the agreement.

***

In January 2015, at the China-CELAC summit, China announced that it would aim to increase China-Latin America trade to five hundred billion, and Chinese investment in Latin America to two hundred fifty billion American dollars by 2025. That is a doubling of the current amount, and most of it will be in the primary commodities.

Many of the already planned projects are cut across some of the region's biodiversity hotspots, national parks, and where ancient people earn their livelihood.

But both Latin American nations and China need to safeguard the social and environmental impacts of this economic activity, for different reasons.
Commodity-led growth is not sustainable from a social and environmental point of view. Commodity-led growth needs to be properly governed so that the government can capture windfalls, and invest them, not only into alternative forms of economic activity, but also into people, and the

environment as well.

For China, it will make sense to upgrade, enforce, and make its social and environmental policies, more transparent on economic and political grounds.

They would help mitigate risk to Chinese companies, and lenders, by strengthening public confidence, in host countries, thus bolstering the position of Chinese banks and recipient governments.

This would also help Chinese firms for future market access. In many Latin American countries, the public record of protests has resulted in delays or denial of contracts.

Environmental-related risks can certainly affect the bottom line of Chinese companies. The large-scale Belo Monte dam project in Brazil is a case in point. Although Brazilian firms dominate the project, State Grid Corporation of China has taken over power distribution.

The project is another example where indigenous communities and environmental concerns have run up high. Massive protests and international scorn over the project are estimated to cost the developers $1.4 million per day and may delay the project for two years. Hence, adopting established safeguards would help Chinese companies, enter other markets as well, even in the industrialised world, where the standards are significantly higher than in Latin America.

***

China has reemerged as a world economic power, in the twenty-fifth century. As it has risen, it has increasingly purchased from and invested in Latin American primary commodities.

Today, China is the number one trading partner for some of the region's largest economies, and China's development banks pour more money into the region than the World Bank, or Inter-American Development Bank (IDB).

China has been guzzling oil from Venezuela, Ecuador, and Mexico to fuel its expanding fleet of cars, trucks, and container ships. China has wired more than half of the world's consumer electronics projects, with copper from Chile and Peru.

Many of China's new cities have iron ore from Brazil at their core. As standards have risen, the Chinese eat more beef, from cattle that are fed soya beans from Argentina, and Brazil. Chinese companies have flocked to the Americas to invest in these commodities, backed by China's state-run development banks.

Chinese trade and investment in primary commodities caused prices and exchange rates to sky-rocket in the region and made Latin American manufacturing industries less competitive on a global scale. Textiles, footwear, car making, and electronics from Argentina, Brazil, Mexico, and Colombian sombreros have lost significant market share in the world and regional markets.

The World Bank puts the economic costs of environmental degradation, during the China Boom at 8.6 per cent of annual GDP, dwarfing the 3,6 annual growth. Mining, oil exploration, and large-scale farming activities often necessitate the clearing of forests and pollution of waterways; they are found in areas where many of the world's richest indigenous cultures reside.

Global advocacy campaigns are also staggering over Chinese oil exploration in the Ecuadorean Amazon and hydroelectric dams near biosphere reserves in Honduras.

Alternatively, Latin American governments fell far short in capturing their China windfall, and investing some of the proceeds into industry and innovation, into people, and into protecting the environment.

China-led commodity boom was amongst the longest and most lucrative in the region. Most of the Latin American nations saved less of these windfalls than they had in past booms. Some analogous studies by the United Nations show that the region's governments also failed to capture fiscal revenue in proportion to the windfall profits, made in the sector, during the China Boom as well.

Also, Latin American taxation systems are not keeping pace with economic activity.

According to Economic Commission for Latin America and the Caribbean (ECLAC), the region's tax is only eighteen per cent of the GDP, compared to 34.3 per cent of the GDP among Organisation for Economic Cooperation and Development (OECD) countries.

The region will need to expand tax bases, by increasing revenues. Moreover, the region relies more on indirect taxes – value-added and export taxes, than on direct taxes on income and wealth.

Of paramount importance, alongside the basic tax system, in the region, is the need to upgrade institutions to capture windfalls from the commodities sector, where fiscal revenue did not increase with the proportion of rents.

Governments across the region will need to reform taxation regimes, as well as systems of royalty payments, and windfall programs for the commodity sector.

In the oil and gas sector, the Latin American government took in thirty-four to seventy-eight per cent of the rents during the China Boom, compared to ten to thirty-five per cent in mining.

Bolivia, Chile, and Peru took bold steps, during the China Boom to increase royalties and taxes, in the mining sector, and took in highs of twenty-seven to thirty-five per cent of mining rents in those countries.

During the earlier part of the China Boom, China upgraded its existing copper stabilisation fund. In 2006, Chile established the Economic and Social Stabilisation Fund (FEES), which takes windfall profits from the copper sector, and is held aside to help fund fiscal deficits, when the copper price is low, or when there is a general economic downturn.

The FEES took in $24.6 billion, allowing Chile, to have one of the larger stimulus packages, in the wake of the 2008-2009 financial global crises.

***

Latin America holds strategic assets to leverage when engaging with China. China, looking to advance its flagship companies overseas, and provide financing to emerging markets to diversify its assets, maybe more willing to engage than it had during the China Boom.
There are three areas, where China may buy into a development strategy in Latin America. First, China will continue to be a source of demand for Latin American commodities, and possibly for a more diversified array of products, if Latin America gets its policies right.

Second, China may become have an even larger presence in terms of foreign direct investment in Latin America. Third, China and its growing set of development banks, and funds, can be a source of much-needed finance for infrastructure, industrialisation, and green development.

While the manufacturing sector in Latin America has lost competitiveness during the commodity boom, the Chinese transformation offers a second chance. If Latin American nations put a premium on innovation, industrialisation, and export competitiveness, they may find openings in the Chinese economy that are not on offer elsewhere. Indeed, in 2014, the Brazilian aircraft giant Embraer signed 2.6 billion dollars' worth of deals to sell small jets to small startup regional airlines in China, showing that demand is picking up for China's new jetting class. Moreover, China's transformation may give Latin American consumers and other manufacturing products, some breathing room in terms of export competitiveness, through the exchange rate channel.

As China becomes more of a consumer society and moves forward on financial reforms, it will ease its grip on the exchange rate. If managed properly, the exchange rate will likely appreciate over the longer run. This will trigger more imports on the Chinese side, and help make Latin American exports more competitive globally as well.

Based on retained earnings from China's domestic boom, and healthy lines of credit, from the likes of the China Development Bank (CDB), and China Export-Import Bank (CHEXIM), Chinese national champions are looking to merge with, or acquire Latin American companies, that will be suffering due to slowdown, lower prices, and bloated balance sheets, due to exchange rate depreciation.

As exchange rates and wages increase in China, Latin America may not be a destination for foreign investment, in the primary commodities sector.

Mexico and Central America will prove to be a platform, to access the US market as the United States gains momentum and those countries become more competitive.

Indeed, Chinese textiles, and copper tubing companies have already relocated to Mexico, and auto companies may soon follow.

Chinese auto companies have already Uruguay, seeking access to the Argentine and Brazilian markets through MERCOSUR.

There is no sign that China is turning off the spigot in terms of finance to Latin American governments, either though it may begin to take different forms.

Since 2005, China's policy banks have provided upward of one hundred nineteen billion American dollars to Latin American governments for infrastructure and mining projects.

In January 2015, China hosted the first China-CELAC (Community of Latin American and Caribbean States) summit and held the first-ever conversation between China and the entire Latin American region.

At that meeting, China pledged to increase trade with Latin America to five hundred billion American dollars, and investment to two hundred fifty billion American dollars by 2025.

To kick start the pledge, China established several funding arrangements totalling thirty-five billion American dollars including twenty billion special loans for China-Latin America infrastructure cooperation, the ten billion preferential loans for Latin American countries as well, and the five billion China-CELAC Cooperation Fund that China promised previously.

The fifty million American dollars China – Latin America Infrastructure Cooperation Special Fund has also started to invest in special projects.

China continues to see overseas finance and foreign direct investment to diversify its holdings of US treaties.

In addition to ramping up investments abroad through the CDB and CHEXIM, China is rapidly setting up new financial vehicles. In addition to the CELAC-China fund, China cofounded the hundred billion American dollars New Development Bank, with BRICS countries in 2015, and the hundred billion Asian Infrastructure Investment Bank.

The CELAC - China forum offers a fresh opportunity for a regional dialogue with China, rather than (or at least to supplement) bilateral economic relations.

If managed properly, this will allow the region to reach common goals, for regional infrastructure, industrialisation, and environmental protection, and then it can then engage with China collectively.
At the China – CELAC summit leaders, from Latin America and China drew up a China – CELAC Cooperation Plan (2015-2019). The plan covers a wide range of issues, including peace and security, international affairs, trade, investment, finance, infrastructure,

transportation, energy, resources, education, culture, sports, and environmental protection.

China – CELAC Cooperation Plan is an unprecedented opportunity for Latin America to upgrade competitiveness, and environmental protection.

In addition to pledging to increase trade and investment, and to create several funding vehicles to facilitate such trade, investment and finance, China, and CELAC pledge to enhance collaboration to promote in CELAC countries, the industrialisation of value-added goods.

There is also a view to supporting the industrialisation and integration of small SMEs in global value chains.

If that isn't enough, the plan also commits to exploring initiatives, for the joint construction of industrial parks, science and technology, special economic zones, and high-tech industrial parks, between China and CELAC countries, especially in research and development (R&D) activities, to improve industrial investment and the forming of the industrial value chain and to explore the possibility of inaugurating the China-LAC Industrial Development and Cooperation Forum in due time.

China also commits to making major investments in Latin American infrastructure, and with a better eye on the sustainability of such projects. China-LAC Cooperation Fund, China-LAC Special Loan for Infrastructure, concessional loans offered by China, as well as other financial resources, to support key cooperation projects between China and CELAC countries, in a manner consistent with the social, economic, and environmental development needs of the CELAC region, as well, with sustainable development vision.

The plan is nothing short of incredible, and offers the best and most balanced opportunity for Latin American economic development, in eighty years. The plan also indicates that Latin American leaders have already come to realise the need to diversify their economies and make economic development more sustainable.

However, the CELAC-China Cooperation Plan is organised and contains many of the exact initiatives, that can be found in the Africa-China Cooperation Plan under the auspices of the Forum on China-Africa Cooperation (FOCAC), negotiated in Beijing in 2012, indicating that it is China that is the motivating force for industrialisation and sustainable development in the region.

The plan also suggests that China and CELAC will cooperate on global climate change negotiations, and invest in more renewable energy in Latin America.

The two have pledged to enhance collaboration in the protection of biodiversity, coastal ecological system, reserves management, environmentally sound technologies, water conservation, desertification combat, pollution control, and treatment, among other issues.

It will be up to Latin American nations in CELAC to make the environment as much of a priority as industrial diversification.

The current pattern of China-Latin America trade and investment is endemic to environmental degradation, high carbon emission, and social conflict. New industry and infrastructure will need to be geared towards structural transformation, which is environmentally sustainable.

One area for cooperation is Latin America's lucrative

clean energy potential. According to the IDB, Latin America will need to double its installed power capacity by 2030 for $4 hundred thirty billion American dollars. The IDB estimates that the region could produce orders of magnitude of more electricity from solar wind, geothermal, and biomass energy sources in Latin America.

For this, infrastructure needs to be thought of in terms of regulatory infrastructure, internet communications, energy, electricity, as well as roadways, railways, and ports. CELAC and China would do well to adopt a strategy like the IDB's Sustainable Infrastructure for Competitiveness and Inclusive Growth. Newly created industrial clusters should be linked with cities, ports, and markets, rather than the old model of simply building roads, to the latest oil, or mining concessions.

Putting clean energy and social environmental safeguards into the core of the CELAC-China economic cooperation agenda is in the interests of both parties.

For China, it would be important that reduces its political and economic risks. Projects that do not include stringent safeguards turn into political and economic nightmares.

And, for Latin America, it would be important to maintain the stock of natural resources for economic growth overall and to maintain the rich cultural and biodiversity that the region enjoys.

***

DRAGON IN AFRICA

Over the next three years, since 2006, during the Beijing Summit of the Forum of China – Africa Cooperation, the Chinese pledged to double aid, ratchet up concessional finance for trade and infrastructure, and allow duty-free entry for many African exports. China would set up a fund for Africa, build a hundred rural schools, and thirty hospitals, and establish up to five trade and economic cooperation zones across the continent. This strategic partnership with Africa would be based on 'win-win' cooperation.

After the Beijing Summit, China was on track to become the African continent's biggest trading partner, outpacing Britain and the United States. Nearly nine hundred Chinese companies had invested in Africa by then – in factories, farms, retail shops, and oil wells. Li Ruogu, head of China's CHEXIM China Export-Import Bank, predicted six months after the summit that this bank would commit twenty billion American dollars over the next three years, to finance Chinese exports, and business in Africa (including North Africa). By comparison, World Bank loan commitments to countries in Africa over a similar three-year period (2006-2008) totalled just over seventeen billion American dollars.

China has given aid to every country in Africa, except one: Swaziland, which alone has never switched allegiance from Taiwan.

Others have condemned China's policy of engaging

with all countries that grant it diplomatic recognition, and its pledge not to interfere in domestic affairs, which means that the leadership actively engages with dictators, shunned by many other governments.

The Chinese press painted a rosy picture, of friendship and mutual benefit. African leaders were uniformly positive about the benefits of the Chinese embrace. Journalists in Africa and the West were much more sceptical.

The Chinese were targeting aid only to countries with rich natural resources, and questionable governance, and giving three times as much aid as the entire West combined. China was tainted as a 'rogue donor', and its aid was called as 'toxic' that hurt ordinary citizens, a highly placed US foreign policy pundit told his audience.

Some claimed that the Chinese were using prison labour, while others predicted that China would manipulate debt relief for political leverage.

***

Zambia's Chambishi copper mine had been closed for more than ten years, when China Non-Ferrous Metals Cooperation (CNMC), bought eighty-five per cent of the mine in 1998, for twenty million American dollars, investing another one hundred thirty million for its rehabilitation. CNMC were its pioneer.

By the end of 2005, more than one hundred sixty Chinese companies had invested in Zambia. A thousand Zambians were employed at Chambishi alone. The Chinese investors had complaints, as a Zambian newspaper, reported: 'the Zambian government's rigid control over expatriate staff, high transportation costs, due to its land locked position, poor infrastructure, discriminatory incentives, complicated labour relation laws, frequent strikes by workers, and poor local industries were not helping investors.'

The Chambishi joint venture marked the start of a steep learning curve for the Chinese. In April 2005, as many as fifty-one factory workers were killed in an explosion at the Chinese-owned BGRIMM explosives plant on the grounds of the Chambishi mine.

The Chinese were widely accused of lax safety standards, and observers looked at the disaster with a high rate of fatalities in China's mines.

The Chinese company paid funeral costs, of some ten thousand American dollars per employee killed, but the BGRIMM explosion also helped facilitate Zambia's National Union of Miners and Allied Workers' efforts, to organise workers at the Chinese mine.

The following year, in a protest over wages, workers on the night shift at Chambishi vandalized equipment at the mine and attacked the Chinese manager.

The next morning, as a fracas, at the gate, turned into a riot, a worker was shot, and wounded by security guards. When rumours spread that he had been killed, another group of miners stormed the Chinese residential compound, where, apparently, a panicked manager, fired a gunshot and there were other five wounded miners.

The Chinese connection grew into a heated issue in the Zambian presidential election in September 2006. Opposition Patriotic Front candidate Michael Sata, who had visited Taiwan, at the invitation of its government, seized on the anti-Chinese feeling. Aid and investment from China were Trojan horses, he said.

After concerns about local demonstrations, kept then-Chinese President Hu Jintao from visiting Chambishi to inaugurate the Zambia – China Economic and Trade Cooperation Zone, in February 2007, Zambian Minister of Mines, Dr Mwansa, chided the people of Chambishi for their militant stand.

Hu Jintao had promised that China would invest at least eight hundred million American dollars in the Zambia – China economic zone, creating thousands of local jobs. Mwansa reminded the people of Chambishi that copper-processing factories planned by the Chinese would help Zambia to industrialise, and move away, from simply exporting raw copper concentrate.

In July 2007, Mwansa and President Mwanaswasa visited Chambishi to preside over the launch of the Chinese company's new social responsibility plan.

A spokesman for the Chinese firm announced that they were supporting renovations at the Sino-Zam Friendship Hospital (another Chinese aid project), repairing local roads, building bus shelters, and public recreation facilities, and giving money for local education, and women empowerment.

In the past, the Chinese have given more aid to countries, they believed to be fellow travellers on the socialist road: Tanzania, Guinea and even Sierra Leone.

Tanzanian President Julius Nyerere visited China thirteen times. Zhou Enlai declared Africa 'ripe for revolution' during his tour in 1964, and the Chinese gave material support to guerrilla movements in the African bush.

In 1967, inspired by Chinese moves towards collective farming, and by his own ideas about African socialist traditions, Nyerere established a grand project of socialist cooperatives–ujamaa villages, modelled on China's experience.

***

Tanzania and Zambia maybe China's oldest and closest friends in sub-Saharan Africa. Knit together by a long-shared border, the two countries were each led for decades by charismatic African socialists, who bequeathed them legacies of stability, peace, and broad-based poverty.

At the height of the chaos of the Cultural Revolution, China's premier Zhou Enlai offered to build Africa's longest railway, nearly two thousand kilometres, stretching from the copper mines of land locked Zambia through Tanzania to the sea.

The enormous and costly railway project had been envisioned by Cecil Rhodes, in the late nineteenth century, and briefly considered by the British colonialists half a decade later.

In the lead-up to independence, the man who would become Zambia's first president. Kenneth Kaunda, called again for the railway line to be built; it was rejected as infeasible by a World Bank mission.

Although a consortium of British and Canadian firms, disagreed, they were unable to raise financing for the project. Germany also declined.

In 1967, Tanzania, Zambia and China signed off the project, to widespread scepticism.

Construction began in 1970, finishing in 1975, two years ahead of schedule. This enormous railway line, with ten kilometres of tunnels, and three hundred bridges, still dwarfs any other infrastructure project to date, in China's current wave of economic engagement in Africa.

For decades afterwards, the world knew of China's aid program through the Tan Zam railway. Many were surprised to learn that China had done anything else in Africa.

In China, the railway project continues to represent the pinnacle of the kind of struggle, hardship and glorious achievement pushed by Mao. The language of sacrifice parallels the tales of Daqing's Iron Man, or the energetic (if over-aided) agricultural brigade at Dazhai.

In 2006, China's 'Year of Africa' the Chinese media made sure that the history of the Tan Zam railway was known in every Chinese home.

A China Central Television (CCTV) show on Africa and China featured an interview with a veteran of the railway construction: 'Sometimes, we had to drink the water that we found in the elephants footprints,' he said.

A journalist from China's official news agency Xinhua reported: 'Food was shipped from China, but the half-month voyage meant they were confined to eating dehydrated vegetables.

'Even soy sauce was a luxury. Sometimes, when supplies arrived, the wheat flour had gone mouldy. Living in tents in the wilderness was dangerous, too. They had to check their shoes for snakes, before putting them on in the morning. At night they could hear lions roaring outside.'

By 1972, China had committed aid to twenty-nine countries in Africa 1973. In 1978, seventy-four countries were receiving aid from China, the largest group of them in Africa.

By then, China had aid programs in more African countries, than in the United States.

For a time in the 1970s, a more confident Third World seemed to be rising. Votes from African countries enabled communist China to finally be seated at the United Nations in 1971.

***

At the end of December 1982, Chinese premier Zhao Ziyang headed to Africa to 'advance exploringly' (as his translator put it) on the path of South-South cooperation. He visited eleven countries on a trip that lasted over four weeks.

Zhao was greeted like a visiting rock star. Cheering throngs lined the streets of his motorcade. In Zimbabwe, five thousand people, waited at the airport, to greet the Chinese leader. They stampede onto the runway when security officials opened the gate an hour before Zhao was due to arrive. Five women were trampled to death, sixty-four people were injured, and scores fainted in the crush.

At a press conference in Dar es Salaam, the seaside capital of Tanzania, Zhao announced that four sets of principles – equality and mutual benefit, stress on practical results, diversity, in form, and common progress, which would guide the new China as it worked out its economic relations with other developing countries.

Although many of the details of Zhao's four principles

echoed the eight principles announced by Zhou Enlai, in 1964, Zhao did not mention the word aid.

He emphasised instead that cooperation with African countries would take a variety of forms, undertaking construction projects, entering cooperative production, and joint ventures.

Zhai explained that cooperation would build capacity and foster growth in China as well as in Africa and that each side could complement the other. Beijing Review, China's authoritative English language magazine, pointed out to foreigners that four principles of cooperation were a significant chance.

Over time, China planned to switch the emphasis away from aid, and toward a variety of other forms of engagement that would benefit both partners. Economic cooperation between poor countries cannot be sustained, the magazine concluded, if it is limited to one-way aid.

Zhao's four-week trip was every bit as historic for Africa, as Zhou Enlai's trip had been almost twenty years earlier, although it aroused much less alarm (or even interest) in the West. It sent a strong signal that China wanted to remain engaged in Africa, as China's adjustment was underway.

In the 1980s, the demands of China's modernisation meant that ties with Europe, the United States, and Asia predominated for economic engagement, but aid policy continued to favour Africa, over other regions.

As the dean of China-Africa studies at the University of Illinois, Professor George Yu, observed in 1988, 'China's interest in and relations with Africa have persisted and expanded'.

As China's economy recovered from the initial jolt of adjustment, aid rose again. According to a study published by the Development Assistance Committee (DAC), of the OECD, in 1984, China was the eighth largest bilateral donor in sub-Saharan Africa, with commitments very close to those made by Norway, and not far below Japan, and the United Kingdom.

China would go on to direct an average of fifty-seven per cent of its foreign aid, to Africa between 1986 and 1995. Aid to Africa would increase, even as it dropped, in other significant regions, such as Asia.

This gave China a steady presence, credibility, and a strong foundation that Beijing would build on in the years after 1995.

China also reformed its standard operating procedures for aid, adding more rigorous economic analysis, to the feasibility studies they did before they agreed to do a project.

In 1982, Liberia's government asked China to rehabilitate Barrake, a sugarcane plantation and factory near the remote coastal town of Buchanan.

They expected a prompt affirmation. Instead, the Chinese sent a fifty-man team to do a lengthy feasibility study. The team concluded that sugar production at Barrake would need an annual subsidy of 3.6 million. Liberia should look for a more profitable project. Another reform targeted the weak local capacity.

Brain drain, economic crises, and poaching of staff by

donor agencies robbed African governments of personnel with management and technical skills needed to run projects.

The Chinese government had been giving scholarships for African students to study in China, but most project training had been done on-site.

Now aid officials were authorised to send medium and high-level African staff to China, for six months, to a year, to develop management and technical skills, and the Chinese set up a fund, for African human resource development to pay these expenses.

And, Chinese also expanded the existing system of counter-trade (barter) to encompass their former aid projects.

***

In 1984, China's Mali embassy arranged for a Chinese company to rescue a state-owned leather factory project originally established as a Chinese aid project. The company provided commercial credit with deferred payment, allowing the factory to order spare parts, and upgrade its production equipment.

The Malian company paid them in kind by exporting cattle hides – something it had in abundance. China had used barter arrangements in Africa as long as the 1960s, swapping Chinese goods, for Africa's raw materials.

China's aid projects could use the products they produced to repay loans for working capital, spare parts, or even the original aid loan. This enabled aid recipients to avoid using scarce foreign exchange.
There is a lot of resemblance between these resource credit swaps to arrangements used by China, in Angola, DRC

(Congo), and elsewhere in Africa, in recent years.

These arrangements were widely in place in the late 1980s.

As Taiwanese researcher Chang Lin pointed out in 1993, the expanding practice of countertrade was transforming China into a new and large buyer of primary products, one who is willing to supply development goods and services, in return for local products, such as coffee from Ghana, copper from Zambia, and so on.

Tanzania bought spare parts for Chinese projects by exporting cashew nuts. Sierra Leone exported coffee and cocoa to make some of its loan payments.

Similarly, Angola would use oil, Senegal's peanut oil, and Ghana, cocoa, to repay their loans.

***

Throughout the lost decade of the 1980s, and well into the 1990s, China focused the bulk of its aid on rehabilitating the dozens of former aid projects, that had collapsed, or was barely limping along, and developing ways to make their initial benefits sustainable.

For every new project launched during this period, three were consolidated (repaired, renovated, and reconditioned). The first step in the consolidation policy was a decision in 1983, to send teams to Africa, to survey former aid projects and determine their need for spare parts. In Tanzania, the Chinese signed an agreement to renovate more than sixty former aid projects.

Hydropower stations built under Chinese aid earlier, such as the seventy-four-megawatts Bouenza project in the Congo, received complete overhauls. Upgrading and repairing completed projects was less visible, and even less rewarding.

Chinese officials complained mildly that it was more complicated than the new construction, but they persisted. Being responsible to the end became a new slogan for aid.

There was one major complication. China's approach to aid had been tightly bound by a strict interpretation of the hallowed foreign policy principle: China would not interfere in other countries' internal affairs. This created what one researcher called a sovereignty trap.

Chinese experts could construct a project, they could train local people, how manage an irrigation system, or produce textiles, in a factory.

But, until this point, they never involved themselves directly in management. This was seen as 'interference in their host's internal affairs.

And yet, on average one out of every six turnkey projects, needed a Chinese team, to return after the project ended, to advise or conduct further training.

Release from the sovereignty trap would not allow China to offer, not just technical assistance but also management assistance for their former aid projects. Because this was seen as a political issue, the decision had to come from the highest level: Premier Zhao Ziyang. He declared that offering management and technical cooperation for completed projects was not interfering in internal affairs, 'but helping them to build self-reliance.' This tide turned. Soon, Chinese teams implementing turnkey projects were required to propose the idea of long-term partnerships, to the recipient country.

The idea of Chinese managers in state-owned enterprises was also viewed with distaste by some African leaders, such as Julius Nyerere, who believed it to be an infringement of sovereignty.

It was also resisted by those African officials who relied on being able to dole out jobs, in state-owned factories, as a key element of their patronage system. Nonetheless, when Zhao brought up the idea in his 1982-3 African trip, some governments agreed to try it.

Sierra Leone was a test case. The Magbass sugar complex was completed in 1982, and became the first Chinese aid project in Africa, to immediately hire Chinese experts as managers, and pay them from the company's profits.

However, it was Mali that became a laboratory for the Chinese to study and adjust to the new practice.

The state-owned sugar factory built by the Chinese, but handed over to the Malians, a decade earlier, appointed Chinese experts, as general managers and heads of all departments.

The Chinese directly controlled personnel, finance, and materials. These changes raised output by almost a hundred per cent. In 1989, L'Essor, a Malian newspaper, praised this innovative cooperation policy, as unmatched, in West Africa. The Malians asked for Chinese experts to run the rest of the five factories, formerly set up by the Chinese aid program.

Having Chinese managers also helped China in its goal to consolidate its former aid projects. The five Malian factories paid the cost of the eighty-four Chinese experts, and their airfare, saving us a lot of foreign exchange, the deputy director of China's Department of Foreign Aid commented in 1988.

Some of the Malian factories began to earn foreign exchange through exports. They paid upfront for imported spare parts, and new machinery from China, and began repaying their aid loans.

China's search for ways to consolidate its projects and ensure that new ones thrived was an effort to face the situation. But, ultimately, providing Chinese managers and providing new loan funding for rehabilitation was not enough to ensure sustainability.

As a Chinese researcher pointed out in the case of Tanzania, China's management teams could not leave even more than ten years after the transfer of the enterprise, not because of the need to pass on the skills, but due to the inability of the Tanzanian enterprises, to survive and develop their own.

Chinese-built projects became a burden on the backs of the two governments. Once the Chinese side stopped 'blood transfusion,' the projects could not operate properly. Efficiency declined, machines became worn out, and finally, the whole project became paralyzed.

Chinese managers even faced more limitations in Sierra Leone. Problems with local corruption limited the Magbass factory's ability to cover its operating costs or repay the loan, as the Chinese hoped.

Local staff members regularly stole large quantities of the cane alcohol distilled at the plant. Politicians expected gifts of hundred kgs of bags of sugar whenever they visited the factory.

The government of Siaka Stevens fixed the factory's sale price for sugar, at about a third of the retail price. The Chinese told me this ex-factory price was below their production costs). The government then gave an exclusive contract to market the sugar to a well-connected local businessman, who pocketed the difference.

Problems like those at Magbass and Kpatawee, pushed the Chinese to begin to explore the links between aid and investment. China would never impose privatisation as a condition for assistance. However, privatisation entered as one of a portfolio of ways to resuscitate failed projects, restoring them to life, and sometimes health.

***

China's coastal province of Fujian established the Fujian-Africa Fishing Company, in the early 1980s.

They approached as many as forty African countries, between 1981, and 1984, in a quest to negotiate fishing rights and develop joint ventures. As a trial effort to nurture joint ventures between Chinese companies and those in Sierra Leone, China set up a fund of about ten million American dollars in 1985.

The first wave of Chinese joint ventures in Africa began in a small way in 1981, when two Chinese companies tentatively invested six hundred sixty hundred American dollars in joint ventures, worth about three million American dollars.

By 1985, the Chinese government had signed off on

twenty-seven small and medium Chinese investments in Africa totalling twenty-four million, with the Chinese holding more than half of the equity.

Uncertain about the local ways, the first Chinese companies to venture into African investments preferred arrangements where their local partners could take the responsibility for managing government relations and paying taxes and other fees.

During the difficulties of the civil war, the Fujian company sold its shares to the China National Fisheries Company in Beijing.

But, the sixteen boats of the joint venture, continued to fish in the coastal waters of the Gulf of Guinea. The Chinese partners provided the vessels and took fifty-one per cent of the venture. They built a refrigerated bonded warehouse, and a repair shop, and retained forty-nine per cent of the profits.

Each vessel carried fifteen men. The captain, engineer, boatswain, and first mate are still Chinese. Ten sailors are local.

Fishing with industrial fleets raised new risks for overfishing. They might also compete with the traditional fishermen in the shallower waters along the coast. To reduce these threats, each ship also includes a government observer, from Sierra Leone Marine Resources, who radios in the latitudes and information of the catches, in the country's modest effort to monitor fishing, in its territorial waters.

The venture has been profitable over the decades, but today's time seems hard. Security is poor on the seas.

Pirates hit tens of the boats. They beat up the crew, took all their apparel, and mobile phones, and siphoned most of their fuel.

In 1987, the Chinese stepped into leasing on a trial basis, with the Mali sugar complex, which they were already managing, and the sugar refinery they had built in Togo.

In 1991, after reviewing the experience with aid-related investment, Beijing allocated money for a special aid diversity fund, to support additional experiments. The fund provides modest, medium-term loans (repayment in one to six years) at low interest, as seed capital for joint ventures in Africa, particularly for joint ventures that would help consolidate projects, that had previously been funded under China's aid. Some African governments were offered soft loans to use (or lend to private firms) as local shares of a joint venture.

Aid-related joint ventures accelerated after this. China's complete Plant Import and Export Corporation (Complant), the company used by the Ministry, to organise the implementation of aid projects, became part owner of a sugar company in Benin.

Mali also used this strategy to partially privatize the Segou Textile Mill built with Chinese aid. The Chinese government sweetened the project with policy support and funding. China National Overseas Engineering Corporation (now known as COVEC) took on eighty per cent of the shares; the Mali government kept twenty per cent.

The value of the shares was deducted from the foreign aid debt Mali owed to China. COVEC agreed to repay the factory's remaining debt, and contributed some of its funding for rehabilitation.

***

In Nigeria and Mali, two Chinese aid teams tentatively took on construction projects for profit that year.

Chinese construction companies began to stick around after building aid projects, used to register as a local company, and then bid on construction projects.

Two years later, Chinese companies were earning hard currency, with projects in nine African countries. The Chinese joined the World Bank in 1980, and the African Development Bank in 1985, which made them eligible to bid on projects financed by these banks.

Chinese companies supplied labour for the Kigali – Ruhengeri Road, funded by German aid in Rwanda, and bid on a World Bank-financed project in Rwanda.

In Africa, the construction business looked promising at the start of the 1980s.

But, after several years, Africa's economic crises had deepened, structural adjustment policy loans were on the rise, and the decline in infrastructure spending by other donors created difficulties for China's new overseas construction companies.

Drawing on Chinese aid funds enabled Chinese companies to generate business, offering a friendly project and a friendly price.

It was a winning bid to construct staff housing at a Gambian hospital. The Gambians hired a team of five

Chinese to keep running their seventeen thousand-seat stadia. The place was a dormitory for athletes during matches, and when no matches were scheduled, it was a hotel, that helped repay the loan.

African nations receive about fourteen billion American dollars in assistance from foreign countries. Chinese enterprises hope that they can make profits through contracting more projects involving this foreign aid.

***

In Banjul, the capital of Gambia, nine Chinese experts from the China Building Material Company, and a group of Gambians building a small factory produced bricks.

China paid for the airfare for the nine experts, the Gambia paid about two hundred dollars a month for each as a living allowance, and the UN Capital Development Fund (UNCDF) paid the rest of the costs.

China and the UN Family Planning Association created a similar arrangement to build a maternity clinic in the Gambia. Chinese aid officials liked these tripartite projects because they were low-cost, usually had quick results, and stretched China's aid resources. These projects had increased dramatically in recent years, and it had become a norm of foreign assistance.

In just two years, 1986- 1987, China was able to undertake forty-four small projects, twenty-three in Africa, with various United Nations agencies, on a tripartite basis.

A 1983 road project in Somalia co-financed with the African Development Bank, and the World Bank, and discussions with the Canadian Agency for International

Development on co-financing an agricultural project in Rwanda, demonstrated that China was at least open to tripartite cooperation with other donors.

In Yemen, the Chinese joined with the Arab Fund to finance a gymnasium in Aden, and China State Construction Engineering Corporation carried out the work.

***

Aid-linked experiments blossomed like a hundred flowers around Africa, in the 1980s and 1990s. However, China's aid changed in other ways. For example, like other countries, they began to use the state-controlled Red Cross to channel some humanitarian aid in disaster situations. It was the African famine of the mid-1980s that pushed the Chinese into a more visible role as a donor of humanitarian aid.

In the early 1980s, it stopped raining in stretches of the dry African Sahel and regions north of the equator. Drought and hunger spread from Ethiopia to Mauritania. Farmers sold their animals, ate their seeds, and then began to starve.

Rural families started the slow, sad trek to towns, where they might find food. NGOs, in the west, mobilised, and this time so did the Chinese Red Cross, making donations to the Central African Republic, Ethiopia, Senegal, Gambia, in 1983, and Lesotho in 1984, when the rains also failed in southern Africa.

In 1985, the Chinese Red Cross raised nearly five million dollars from Chinese citizens, for famine relief. Two more developments in the 1980s would be far more influential in shaping the evolution of aid in China.

It was ratcheting up the diplomatic competition with Taiwan, and China's decision to join the World Trade Organisation.

In 2000, China was starting to harvest the fruits of nearly two decades of reform in its aid and economic relations with Africa. Buildings financed by China's aid, or built by Chinese contractors had reshaped the skylines of dozens of African cities. In Ethiopia, Rwanda, and elsewhere, Chinese contractors, who had originally arrived to carry out Chinese aid projects, were now winning half or more of the construction contracts funded by other donors.

Dar es Salaam alone had eight resident Chinese engineering companies, which had won more than one hundred seventy small and large contacts between 1990 to 1997. A total of 42,393 Chinese engineers and skilled labourers were working in Africa in 2000. China's Ministry of Commerce approved fifty-seven Chinese investments in Africa that year, bringing the total number to just under five hundred. Two-way trade between China and Africa surpassed ten billion dollars. All this happened without much comment from the West.

The launch of the Forum on China –Africa Cooperation (FOCAC), in October 2000 happened one month later when then-Chinese President Jiang Zemin attended the UN Millennial Summit in New York.

Forty-four African countries sent their foreign ministers and those responsible for economic affairs to Beijing.

Much like the FOCAC summit held in Beijing, in 2006, the first FOCAC meeting contained pledges that China would establish an array of new programs – debt relief, training programs, and an investment fund to move its economic co-operation with Africa forward.

Also, in 1995, a clear mandate came down to the Ministry of Commerce from China's State Council: combine aid to Africa, mutual co-operation, and trade together. The strategy was called the 'Great' or 'Mega' Economic and Trade Strategy. The point was simple. Aid would be used to foster three kinds of initiatives, all growing out of the experiments of the 1980s, and early 1990s.

Joint Venture investments in manufacturing and agriculture were first on the list. Assembly factories were a second target. Set up by Chinese companies in Africa, they would create demand for exports of Chinese machinery and parts, as well as fabric and other inputs.

As the government put it in 1995: 'Chinese trade cooperations and manufacturing enterprises should be encouraged to invest in African countries with better investment climate to promote the export of medium and small equipment, processing machinery, relevant technology, and labour service.

Vehicle assembly factories were set up with concessional loans in Cote d'Ivoire, Cameroon, and elsewhere. Finally, the government emphasised exploration and investment in mineral and forest resources. In 1996, long before the war in Darfur erupted, Sudan became the first country to receive Chinese aid to finance oil exploration, in a joint venture with China National Oil Corporation.

The new aid program was deliberately shaped to assist Chinese firms to enter an unfamiliar region, with daunting challenges.

***

As Chines companies became more independent, they did not seem interested in seeking business in Africa. They still saw Africa as Europe's backyard. Just as importantly, China's traditional partners in Africa were alarmed at the change in aid policy, and unsure what it would mean for them.

The Chinese government had a lot of ideas for what Chinese companies should do: they should come to Africa and do intensive studies of local markets.

If the industry was exporting machinery, they should set up repair and maintenance shops to guarantee that customers' needs would be taken care of.

If Chinese medicine, companies should take care to translate directions into English and French. For their part, the Chinese government adopted a multifaceted approach to promote their new strategy and market it to African leaders.

The state-owned Bank of China was directed to set up a branch office in Zambia in 1997, and China Construction Bank opened an office in Johannesburg in October 2000, to make it easier for Chinese companies to enter unfamiliar territory.

Eximbank began offering preferential loans to construction firms in 1998 to boost their ability to win contracts overseas in the Middle East, South Asia, and Africa. Eximbank followed this by opening overseas branches in Cote d'Ivoire and South Africa.

The State Council also directed China's state-owned

companies to launch several trade, investment, and development centres across Africa.

Each centre was to be built and operated independently by an experienced Chinese company with extensive business interests in that country. The centres offered bonded warehouses for traders, referrals for legal assistance, travel, and banking advice, and help with the complicated matters of customs clearance.

In December 1995, Complant newly independent from the Ministry, opened the first trade, investment, and development centre in Guinea, China is a first aid recipient. At least ten other centres followed.

This was a potent symbol of the shift in priorities. The centres were constructed on a standard 'built operate transfer' model. For example, in Benin, the Chinese government contributed a grant of RMB seventeen million (2.5 million American dollars) out of its aid budget to build the five-floor centre, while Zhejiang Tianshi International Economic and Technical Cooperation Company did the design and construction.

In a pattern that would become standard for the mix of aid and business, the Chinese company financed a share of the cost (about a quarter, in Benin case) in return for the right to run the centre for fifty years, after which it would be turned over to the host country.

Additionally, the Ministry directed its municipal and provincial branches to organise delegations of 'outstanding enterprises' to travel to Africa, exposing them to opportunities on the ground.

A delegation from Yunnan province visited Djibouti in

December 1995 and discussed setting up a tobacco farm, and a public-private partnership with the state-owned electricity facility.

One of the Yunnan companies on this delegation later won a contract to manage Djibouti's Sheraton Hotel. In 2007, Guangdong province organised a business seminar in Dar es Salaam, attended by nine hundreds of Chinese business people.

Three Chinese vice premiers fanned out to visit a total of eighteen African countries, in 1995.

Then Chinese premier Li Peng visited Morocco that year, and the following year then President Jiang Zemin travelled to six African countries, the first time a Chinese president ever visited Africa.

***

In early 2008, the rains were late in northern Namibia. Between 2004, and 2008, as Swiss anthropologist Gregor Dobler reported, the number of Chinese shops in the border town of Oshikango quadrupled.

Namibians had allowed the Chinese traders to open their shops on Sundays. In Dar es Salaam, Chinese traders were increasingly visible in the busy central market neighbourhood of Kariakoo.

Their small crowded shops sold traditional medicine, hair pieces, embroidered fabrics, and other Chinese goods. Some Chinese traders were even competing with the village women, squatting on the ground selling groundnuts, and roast corn outside the fish market, and the bus terminal, enticing customers with Swahili shouts of 'Kranga….kranga…kranga! Koni…koni…koni!'

In the 1990s, Chinese products and Chinese traders became a rapidly growing part of the landscape in African cities and rural towns. Many established larger, more formal shops to import Chinese vehicles, machinery, electronics, and equipment. Chinese companies were encouraged to sell and service small power tillers and other kinds of agricultural machinery, first introduced through aid programs.

In addition, with aid projects, at one time, or another, in every country in Africa, but Swaziland and teams of Chinese labourers imported to work on these projects, some stayed behind.

Drawing on *guanxi* (connections) to set up an import business was a fairly easy way to finance the first stage of plans that generally went far beyond a small market stall (or a patch of ground on which to sell groundnuts).

This accelerated after emigration rules were somewhat relaxed in China in 1985.

The pattern of Chinese presence in the African market is partly due to the success of Chinese programs to push Chinese export business to expand into Africa, but there is no evidence that the Chinese government sends workers to Africa under a plan to have them remain behind as traders. These are individual decisions.

***

In May 2007, the China Development Ban launched the first phase of the China – Africa Development Fund (CADF), an equity fund that is expected over time to provide five billion American dollars in finance for ventures by Chinese firms.

The fund will encourage joint projects between state-owned or private Chinese firms, and African companies. The fund will be intended to invest in commercial principles.

That is the reason Chinese policy makers regard entering Africa as entering a new era. They think Africa has gotten rid of some of the major problems such as tribal problems and apartheid struggles, and that they are now concentrating on economic development.

The African market is new, and many companies are not familiar with it, so they need to share the risk with other investors. Most Chinese companies do not have much experience in risk management. At the point of the launch of the fund, the policy makers believed that China-Africa Development Fund would have a longer time horizon than most equity funds, by staying in a project for five to eight years.

The fund planned to invest between five to fifty million American dollars for each project, in minority shareholdings. For this China Development Bank moved quickly to get the fund up and running. By the time the China Africa Development Fund was launched in June 2007, the bank had already sent twenty teams to Africa to set up temporary offices, build relationships, and scout out investment projects in agriculture, manufacturing, electricity, transportation, telecommunications, urban infrastructure, and resource exploration. The first few projects funded included a glass factory in Egypt, a gas-fired power plant in Ghana (a joint venture with a Ghanaian firm) and a chromium processing plant in

Zimbabwe.

The team running the fund, a year later, had moved into posh new quarters, in China's financial district.

The CADF board had approved funding for twenty projects, worth about two billion American dollars, by the end of 2008, and were evaluating more than a hundred other proposals.

Although Africa equity funds have been launched by private firms in industrialised countries, the China-Africa Development Fund has no real counterpart in the efforts by governments of industrialised countries, to foster economic development in Africa.

At a point in time, China's fund was criticised at first because participation was restricted to Chinese companies and their African joint venture partners. But the Chinese listened and decided to open the fund.

At a dinner for a visiting delegation from China-Africa Development Fund, China's ambassador to Liberia, Zhou Yuxiao, told Liberians that the fund's interest in Liberia might be a turning point in the two countries' economic relations.

***

At the Addis Ababa ministerial meeting of FOCAC in 2003, Chinese leader Wen Jiabao promised to give zero tariff treatment to an unspecified number of exports from Africa's least developed countries. The list of commodities and degree of local content stipulations (rules of origin) was negotiated in 2004. The full list of one hundred ninety products was announced in each country in early 2005. At the Beijing Summit in November 2006, the Chinese pledged to increase the list of four hundred forty commodities. This went into effect in July 2007.

China's program was said to cover almost all the exports from the least developed countries. However, a list of goods was not easy to obtain, and this made it difficult to evaluate the potential development impact. China's Minster of Commerce Chen Deming commented that the program removed import tariffs on 'farm products, stone materials, minerals, leather, hide, textiles, clothing, electric appliances and machinery and equipment,' from thirty-one of Africa's least developed countries. He said that between 2006 and 2008, the program had transferred six hundred eighty million in tariff exemptions to thirty-one countries.

Chinese companies have a set of separate incentives for agricultural and natural resource investments. Together, these incentives have stimulated new investment not only in copper, (as in the Democratic Republic of the Congo), but in crops.

Chinese entrepreneurs have begun to plant sesame seeds in Senegal to export duty-free to China, for example. Although, China was continuing to protect its cotton farmers, by not allowing duty-free entry of raw cotton, cotton products from the least developed countries were being allowed duty-free.

According to the Beijing office of the British Department for International Development, the value of exports from Africa to China increased by an average of one hundred and ten per cent. Thirty-two countries in Africa showed an increase in earnings from exports to China, while exports from the remaining twenty had either decreased or showed no change.

We have read repeatedly that Chinese rarely employ locals in their projects. Chinese projects do routinely use more of their nationals as staff, and skilled technicians, than projects carried out by companies from any other country.

They often set up self-contained compounds and live apart from local people. Yet the idea that the Chinese always bring over planeloads of their workers and do not employ Africans is wrong.

Construction of the famous Tan Zam Railway employed some sixteen thousand Chinese at its peak (but many tens of thousands of Africans).

In the Fouta Djallon highlands of Central Guinea, where three of West Africa's mightiest rivers, the Niger, Senegal, and The Gambia, have their headwaters, two hundred Chinese engineers and technicians laboured for two and a half years, besides four hundred and seventy Guineans to build the three-megawatt Kinkon dam on the Kokolou River.

 In 1980, a rice project in The Gambia had forty-five Chinese technicians, while a similar World Bank project hired only three expatriates.

While seventy per cent were sent to work in Asia (including Hong Kong), one hundred fourteen thousand Chinese have been working in Africa, including North Africa.

Algeria and Sudan hosted more new Chinese workers in 2007 than any other African countries. South Africa, with at least, a hundred thousand Chinese, is a prime destination. A range of estimates suggests that anywhere from three hundred thousand to seven hundred fifty thousand people from mainland China have come to work in Africa, since the 1990s, some settling permanently. Any frequent visitor to Africa will notice that there are more Chinese on the streets, and in the towns, than in previous decades.

The reality also is that the ratio of Chinese workers to locals varies enormously, depending on how long a Chinese company has been working in a country, how easy it is to find skilled workers locally, and the local government's policies on work permits.

In Sudan, where Chinese companies have been working in the oil industry, for over a decade, ninety-three per cent of workers in China's oil operations were said to be Sudanese.

A Chinese aid project constructing village water systems, employed about fifty Chinese engineers, technical staff, and about five hundred local workers.

Ultimately, African governments are also the ones in control of the issue of Chinese labour in their countries. Angola requires all employers to have at least seventy per cent of Angola staff. The DRC insisted that at least eighty per cent of the workers in China's multibillion-dollar infrastructure and mining venture must be Congolese.

*****

Under the 2006 FOCAC pledges, the Chines promised to provide short-term training to fifteen thousand African workers.

These short-term training courses in poverty reduction, new leather technologies, and a host of other areas are not linked to specific projects and will do little to build capacity.

Chinese premier Wen Jiabao announced in September 2008, that over the next five years, China would train fifteen hundred principals, and teachers, for the schools it was building in Africa, and thousand doctors, nurses, and managers, for the health sector in the thirty African countries receiving new hospitals from China.

However, vocational training in Africa is a new thrust of China's aid-financed construction. In Ethiopia, a large training and vocational education centre financed by Chinese aid, and jointly operated by the two countries opened in early 2009.

The school will eventually enrol three thousand students, with courses to be taught by Chinese and Ethiopian teachers in construction skills, architecture, engineering, electronics, electrical engineering, computers, textiles, and apparel – all areas of interest to the several hundred Chinese companies now operating in Ethiopia. China also built and operates a vocational training centre in Uganda, and the Chinese are building two centres in Angola.

In addition, the pledge to provide university scholarship programs for four thousand Africans between 2006 to 2009, to earn degrees in China will help build capacity, at the higher levels important for sustainable improvements. At the MDG Summit, in 2008, Premier Wen Jiabao pledged another ten thousand university scholarships, for developing countries over the next five years. Africans with degrees from Chinese universities may be less marketable overseas, and thus very likely to participate in the brain drain to the wealthy countries, at least for a while.

Chinese firms are setting up training institutes in Africa to address local skill shortages they have identified for their projects and business plans. China's major telecoms company, Huawei has established training centres in Angola, South Africa, Nigeria, Egypt, Tunisia, and Kenya, to train Africans in skills needed to operate and maintain wireless telephones and broadband Internet systems.

Some Chinese companies are building African capacity in manufacturing. Nigerians, hard at work, in a local plastic factory, had been using technical experts from China for more than six years. The Chinese transfer their technology, monitor it and then supervise it.

The Chinese continue to return to repair and rehabilitate former projects, sometimes because of their political importance, sometime because they might now turn into a business venture. They work rapidly, using a lot of skilled Chinese workers, but they usually employ more Africans.

***

An African scholar concludes that there is no evidence that Chinese firms will use sub-Saharan Africa as a manufacturing base.

However, South African unions blame a tsunami of Chinese clothing imports for the loss of sixty-seven thousand jobs in their textile industry, while a Nigerian scholar accuses the Chinese of deliberately following a 'policy of deindustrialisation' in his country.

Umar Sani Marshal, a Nigerian industrialist, said that his northern city of Kano was being rejuvenated by growing

Chinese investment in plastics manufacturing.

The highest number of private employers in Kano are Chinese, and they have been expanding day by day. Kenyan political scientist Michael Chege argued that the flood of Chinese imports had not crushed Kenya's manufacturing sector, which was growing at rates as high as seven per cent in 2007.

The impact of competition with Chinese textile exports has been severe for African fabric factories.

Africa's apparel export industry was also badly hit by a wave of competition from Chinese garments. But, at least until the global financial crisis hit in 2008, there was a positive aspect in the rebound of some African garment exporters (Lesotho, Mauritius, Kenya). And, in some regions, in some sectors, contacts between Chinese and African entrepreneurs have helped to catalyse an industrial revolution.

By the turn of the millennium, mainland Chinese companies had already sunk their money into two hundred and thirty different manufacturing projects across Africa. This investment was highly uneven, with Africa's more developed countries – South Africa, Nigeria, Kenya, and Mauritius, accounting for the bulk.

But, as we have seen, the Chinese government has ratcheted up its policy of encouraging Chinese companies to move into manufacturing in Africa.

In 2005, a survey of one hundred fifty Chinese firms with overseas investment projects found that Africa accounted for nearly twenty per cent of the projects; almost half of those (twenty-three projects) were in manufacturing.

Some of China's largest industrial firms are setting up plants in Africa. At the same time, small factories owned by new Chinese investors are multiplying.

Peng Yiyun, a forty-eight-year-old entrepreneur from Baoding, is one of these new investors. In 2000, Peng developed a vegetable farm in Kenya and found a rich reward in the combination of fertile soil, a favourable climate, and high prices in local markets.

He scouted for other opportunities, and in 2003, he returned to Baoding, bought an entire candle factory, and shipped the whole lot to Kenya. Within three years, Peng was producing seven hundred to eight hundred tons of candles in his region. He went back to Baoding, in 2006, to buy machinery for a second factory, this time to process farm products.

***

China's first aid project in Africa was a factory that allowed Guinea to manufacture cigarettes out of its tobacco.

In keeping with the mainstream development ideas, China's initial wave of aid in the 1960s and 1970s focused on the light industry: factories to allow countries to process their natural resources and substitute for imports.

Cigarette factories processing local tobacco were popular. In addition to the Guinea project, China built cigarette (and match) factories in Benin, Mali, Somalia, and Tanzania.

Africa also had a comparative advantage in cotton production, and the Chinese built at least eight major cotton spinning and weaving factories in Africa.

Several countries received tanneries and shoe factories (Mali, Tanzania). Chinese aid projects in agro-processing (rice mills, maize flour, groundnut oil, palm oil, tea) were common.

Sugar factories (usually with a plantation attached, as in Magbass) were also in demand. China built eight large sugar complexes in this first wave of aid. Teams of Chinese also put their stamp on an assortment of other kinds of factories: building materials (bricks, stone crushing), machine tools, and three that made vaccines or pharmaceuticals.

Not surprisingly, Mali, Guinea, and Tanzania, where Mao felt a kinship with the socialist leaders, were the most favoured in this early period.

In Mali alone, China built factories of sugar, pharmaceuticals, tea, textiles, cigarettes, and matches, a tannery, leather processing, and a large rice mill.

Several large factory projects promised to various countries proceeded to completion in the 1980s, among them the Anie sugar complex in Togo, Cimerwa, Rwanda's first cement plant; the Mulungushi textile factory in Zambia, and an ice factory and fish market in Uganda.

A handful of new aid-funded factories were launched in the 1980s in places like Mozambique (textile, shoes) and Zimbabwe (textiles), which came to independence, later than the rest of Africa. Sometimes, new joint ventures could make use of old aid projects.

In Uganda, a new Chinese – Ugandan joint venture in fishing on Lake Victoria was able to make use of the ice factory in Kampala funded earlier by a soft loan from

China. But, under the pragmatic Deng Xiaoping, China's industrial aid in the 1980s focused more on consolidating or rehabilitating the earlier factories.

Most African governments resisted selling off their state assets until the 1990s, but leasing them was sometimes a different matter. By the late 1980s, Chinese companies were managing or leasing sugar factories, built by Chinese aid in Mali, Sierra Leone, Benin, Togo, and Madagascar. Other state-owned companies returned to pick up the pieces at textile and cement factories.

***

On the outskirts of Dar es Salaam, behind a long wall that stretches the length of a couple of city blocks, a factory compound houses the multiple buildings of Urafiki, the Friendship Textile Factory. In 1969, a reporter for the Black Panther newspaper travelled to Tanzania and wrote admiringly about the factory that China had built during the chaos of the Cultural Revolution.

In 1984, the Tanzanian government asked the Chinese to return and run the factory. In the mid-1990s, when Beijing introduced the new system of foreign aid and concessional loans for joint ventures, Friendship Textile mill seemed a good candidate for a trial run.

The Friendship textile mill is the struggling face of China's earlier aid system, a relic of 1969, under life support from the Chinese government.

Chinese began to increase aid for industrial ventures, financing (among other projects) a new cement plant, a woollen knitting factory in Botswana, an ice-making factory in Cameroon, a copper processing factory in

Zambia, and a pharmaceutical factory in Kenya.

Two aid-funded factories were reportedly set up in Sudan, to produce medical gauze and embroidery, and the Chinese gave aid to establish at least four tractors, and farm machinery assembly joint ventures in an assortment of countries. In Ghana, Chinese aid funded ventures in cocoa processing (Calf International Cocoa) and fishnets and rope (Ghana Shandong Netting Company).

In Cote d'Ivoire in 1997, the Chinese embassy (responding to the call from above, for more joint ventures) played a large role in bringing together two Chinese companies and a local firm as a partner in a joint venture, to set up an automobile assembly plant in Abidjan.

In 1998, Ghana received one of the early Eximbank concessional loans of credit for RMB one hundred fifty million (18.1 million).

The Rawlings government used the loan to fund Ghanaian participation in three private joint ventures with Chinese investors: a gold mine, a fishing net, a ropes factory, and the Calf Cocoa project.

The Calf Cocoa project, built near the Tema industrial estate, was a joint venture between China International Cooperation Company for Agriculture, Livestock and Fisheries (CALF), which held fifty-five per cent, and Caridem Development Company (forty-five per cent).

Another example comes from Namibia. The Northern Tannery project in Ondangwa was planned between 1997 and 2000, around the same time as the projects in Ghana.

Namibia's Minister of Trade and Industry decided to use

the concessional line of credit offered by China's Eximbank in 1997, to construct a tannery in the north of the country, where unemployment was high, and raw hides and skins were said to be plentiful and often tossed away.

***

WARS, DIPLOMACY
&
INJUSTICES

ISIS AND ITS MEN

In al Jafr Prison in Jordan, many men were confined mostly in the same communal cells, and they were bound together by their privations, and by their daily struggle to persevere as religious purists among drug dealers, thieves, and killers.

They shared a common creed, a stern brand of Islam, invented by Maqdisi that was inculcated during endless weeks of confinement. They also possessed an uncommon discipline.

The group behaved as a military unit, with clear chains of authority, and unquestioned obedience to Maqdisi's handpicked enforcer, the scarred, thick-chested man known as Ahmad Fadil al Khalayleh, who preferred to be called 'al-Gharib,' or 'the Stranger,' a nickname he had picked up during his days as a fighter during the Afghan civil war.

Some already were calling him 'the one from Zarqa,' the tough industrial town in northern Jordan where he grew up. The phrase in Arabic is 'Al-Zarqawi.'

Maqdisi told the men what to think, but his number two controlled everything else, how the men spoke and dressed, which books they read, which television shows they watched, whether they accepted or resisted prison dictates, when and how they fought.

In the prison, Maqdisi was known to be mild and agreeable,

a more amiable professor than a beguiling mystic.

At just shy of forty, he had the weary air of an intellectual, who felt he deserved better company, than a few other backward men, who shared his cell.

He freely dispensed religious advice, and the occasional fatwa, or religious ruling, but he preferred spending his time in solitary pursuits, writing essays, and reading the Koran.

On the printed page, Maqdisi was fearless, he became renowned throughout the religious world, for inflammatory books with titles such as Democracy Is a Religion, in which he denounced secular Arab regimes, as anti-Islamic, and called for their destruction.

His work eventually gained such resonance among Islamists that a Pentagon-commissioned study in 2006 would call him the most important new thinker in the jihadi intellectual universe.

Previous Islamist ideologues also had criticised leaders of the Arab world, as corrupt and unfaithful to the religion. The same themes appeared in the writings of Sayyid Qutb, the influential Egyptian thinker, whose work inspired the founders of al-Qaeda. But, in Maqdisi's view, each Muslim bore a personal obligation to act, when confronted with evidence of official heresy. It was not enough for the faithful to denounce corrupt rulers.

Whenever interrogators and agents of their intelligence services visited the prison, Maqdisi would greet them politely, and ask about their families, to the dismay of other prison inmates, who had suffered at the hands of the same men.

He would patiently explain to guards and prison officers, why they and their governments were heretics, buttressing their arguments with quotes from the Koran. However, he would often retreat when challenged, allowing that less severe interpretations of the scripture were also valid.

In the prison, Maqdisi was fond of a young physician, who, though secular, was the only person in the prison with an advanced degree.

But politeness and intellect were poor instruments for commanding men in such a hard place as al Jafr. Maqdisi needed an enforcer.

In Zarqawi, he found the perfect helper: a man with the distinction of being once slavishly devoted and utterly ruthless.

Zarqawi had no capacity for warmth or nuance. The man with a scar did not smile. He did not return greetings from prison employees or engage in their small talk.

Whereas Maqdisi preferred the ethereal world of books and ideas, Zarqawi was purely a physical being, with a muscular frame, that he chiselled through weight lifting, using buckets of stones as barbells. The whispered stories, of his criminal past, made him seem dangerous and unpredictable, a man of action, capable of anything.

He had fought bravely, even recklessly, in Afghanistan, and his reputation for impulsive violence had followed him into prison.

He habitually defied authorities, in the first of the jails where he and others were confined, and he humiliated and brutalised inmates who crossed him, sometimes with fists or crude weapons, and sometimes, it was widely said: sexually.

Once, in a rage, he had grabbed a prison guard by his uniform collar and suspended him from a coat hook. Another time, he instigated a violent protest by inmates armed with crude clubs and swords fashioned from bad frames.

Under Maqdisi's tutelage, Zarqawi's attacks subsided. Zarqawi began memorising the Koran, spending hour after hour reading, or staring blankly with the open volume in his lap. His diffuse rage took on a focus: a fierce single-minded hatred perceived for Allah.

The list started with Jordan's King Abdullah, whom Zarqawi saw as an illegitimate leader of an artificial country, responsible for the unspeakable crime of making peace with Israel.

It also included servants of the regime: the guards, the soldiers, the politicians, the bureaucrats, and countless others, who profited from the current system.

Even prison inmates he denounced as *kafirs*, or disbelievers. To Muslims, the term is no mere epithet; if used in a fatwa, it implies that the person has lost the protection of Islamic law, and can be killed with impunity.

Within the prison, the guards were simply referring to Zarqawi, and his closest followers as al-takfiris – 'the excommunicators.'

At the same time, Zarqawi began taking a stronger hand as a leader, and an enforcer among the Islamist prisoners. He demanded the absolute obedience of the men, and he berated them whenever they skipped prayers or watched television news shows anchored by women, who were not veiled. Despite his harsh manner, he won admirers because of his fearless defiance of prison authority. When the official visitors came to al Jafr, Zarqawi would often ignore them and refuse even to acknowledge their greetings. And he would order his men to do the same.

With time, everyone at al-Jafr knew that he worshipped his mother, and how he became a little boy when he visited. He would prepare for days, scrubbing his clothes in the sink, and tidying up his corner of the cell.

Some inmates knew his love letters to her, and his sisters. Scarcely, a word was mentioned about Zarqawi's wife, Intisar, or their two young children. But, to his mother and sisters, he wrote gushing notes adorned with poems, and hand-drawn flowers in the margins.

The other objects of Zarqawi's exaggerated attention were the sick and injured among his men.

When any of the Islamists fell ill, he put himself in the role of a heroic caregiver, giving up his blankets, and rations, to ensure their comfort. He hovered over prison staff, hectoring them whenever he felt his men were being shortchanged.

The prison staff were particularly struck by the tenderness Zarqawi displayed toward the most fragile of the inmates, the double amputee named Eid Jahaline, the unlucky bomber, who flubbed the attack on a pornographic cinema.

Jahaline, who suffered from a psychological disorder in addition to his physical disfigurement, had always bunked with other Islamist inmates, despite his extreme disabilities.

Zarqawi appointed himself as the man's valet, and assisted him, with his bathing, changing, and feeding. Most days he would simply scoop the legless man in his arms, and carry him to the toilet. The prison staff suspected that the daily ritual had so much to do with Zarqawi's peculiar sense of propriety, as with genuine compassion for his comrade.

Under Islam's strict moral code, exposing a man's naked body to others would constitute both a humiliation and a sin.

As time went on, it was the arrival of winter in 1998 that brought freezing temperatures, as prison officials sought to relieve overcrowding elsewhere in the system. The Islamists remained close together, as always, but now subdue cracks were beginning to show.

Some of the jihadists were openly suggesting that Zarqawi should be the leader, replacing Maqdisi, whose professional demeanour had begun to crumble on some members of the group.

Zarqawi made no move against his mentor, but the feelings of many inmates were quite clear.

Maqdisi's nuanced theological arguments were lost on a high school dropout, and petty criminals, who made up much of the group.

These men preferred someone with tough-guy credentials, like Zarqawi, a brawler, who talked candidly and refused to compromise. As he admitted, Maqdisi was no warrior. Even while living in Arab training camps in Afghanistan, he had given up on learning how to use a gun.

He liked being in charge, and he gradually took on a still more dominant role, with his mentor's blessing, leaving Maqdisi to oversee spiritual matters. For the first time, important people outside the prison were beginning to hear his name.

Maqdisi had many admirers within the Islamist movement's diaspora, from London to Palestinian cities of the West Bank, and some of them were men with resources and extensive connections, throughout the Middle East, North Africa, and Europe.

Now, they were learning through Maqdisi about his impressive assistant, an Afghan veteran of unusual courage and natural leadership ability.

In his childhood, Zarqawi was not very Islamic-minded, and when he joined the jihadist movement, it had become an embarrassment.

He tried scrubbing it off in various ways, including with bleach, but the tattoo would not budge. Finally, he turned to one of his Zarqa relatives, who was visiting the prison with a razor hidden in his clothes.

As Zarqawi sat, the kinsman cut two elliptical lines around the tattoo. He then sliced away the upper layers of the skin. When the tattoo was mostly gone, he closed the wound with crude stitches.

Under the sentence handed down by the judge in Amman, Zarqawi's confinement was to continue for another ten years, until 2009, when the muscular and vital young man would be entering middle age. Yet, the prison officials knew that prison terms in Jordan were rarely what they seemed on paper. A sentence could be drastically shortened, after a change in government, or a perceived need to curry favour with a religious party, or a tribe.

***

It was in the late 1960s when Palestinian guerrillas threatened Jordan's sovereignty. A patchwork of militant groups, drawn from four hundred immigrant groups, and refugees massed in Jordan after three decades of wars, staged attacks on Jordanian troops and tried repeatedly to attack King Hussein.

The monarch launched an offensive that became known as Black September, killing thousands of Palestinian militants, and driving many more into Syria and Lebanon. Heavy clashes spilt into the largely Palestinian town of Zarqa, where the man, who would become known as Abu Musab al-Zarqawi was then a boy of four years.

In the 1980s, it was the regional unrest, which threatened to spill across Jordan's relatively peaceful borders. Thousands of Palestinian youths clashed with Israeli troops in the first intifada, or uprising, while young Jordanian men volunteered, by the hundreds to fight the Soviets in Afghanistan.

Some returned to their villages and prison camps, with military skills and new ideas.

A few, like Zarqawi, formed into groups and began looking for ways to continue the struggle against perceived enemies of Islam.

Like other rulers, Jordan's monarchs sought to contain

the threat by fostering powerful and ruthless intelligence networks, to keep the extremists in check. At the same time, they would co-opt relatively moderate Islamists, by granting them positions of privilege and offering limited political freedoms. Abdullah, like his father, supported the Muslim Brotherhood's role as a moderate opposition force in Jordan. And, like his forebearers, he would look for ways to bolster the informal alliance, by granting occasional favours, and concessions that would benefit the group's leadership politically, and ensure loyalty to the crown.

Just such an opportunity came in March 1999, as the country marked the end of the official forty-day mourning, the period for King Hussein's death.

 In a tradition dating back to Jordan's founding, new kings are expected to declare a general amnesty in the country's prisons, granting royal pardons to inmates convicted of nonviolent offences, or political crimes.

It was a way to clean the slate and score points with important constituencies, from the Islamists to powerful East Bank tribes.

To ensure the maximum political return, members of the Parliament were given the task of nominating release-worthy prisoners and drafting the amnesty's legal particulars. Their list quickly grew to five hundred names, then a thousand, then two thousand. And still, lawmakers pushed for more.

A debate over the names spilt into the open. Whereas the new law excluded anyone convicted of a violent crime or terrorism, some lawmakers wanted to free dozens of detainees, convicted of draft dodging, or conspiring in attacks against Israelis.

Others pushed for pardons for the so-called Arab Afghans, veterans of holy war against the Soviets in Afghanistan, who had formed Islamist cells.

In the end, the list, now with more than twenty-five hundred names, was endorsed by Parliament and sent to the palace for final approval. He king faced a choice of adopting the list or sending it back for weeks of additional debate.

He signed it. Many months would pass before the king would learn that it included certain Arab Afghan fighters from the al Jafr Prison, whose Ikhwan-like zeal for purifying the Islamic faith should have disqualified them instantly.

But, by that time, the obscure jihadist named Ahmad Fadil al Khalayleh had become Abu Musab al Zarqawi.

And, there was nothing that the king of Jordan would do, except tell his aides why didn't someone check the list, in an exasperated but utterly futile pique.

On the evening of March 29, 1999, a caravan of prison vehicles arrived at al Jafr to haul away the first of the Islamist prisoners granted freedom under royal amnesty.

Under the law, the state is obliged to deliver inmates to the town where they were first arrested, so Zarqawi and his mentor, Maqdisi took seats on the van, bound for Amman.

They carried few belongings and release papers that reinstated their rights, as free citizens, able to work, visit, associate, and travel just as any Jordanian citizen.

The Amman's van driver waited until dark, then eased the vehicle through the main gate, past the guards, and machine gun nests, past the drooping, parched palm trees, planted along the driveway, and finally onto the rough asphalt of the highway leading to the capital. For the first time in five years, they were free men.

But, not entirely free. Both men had wives and children they barely knew, families that had scraped by during their confinement, surviving on handouts from relatives. Both were subject to scrutiny, and even harassment from the country's secret police.

And, both were bound to the Islamist brotherhood they forged together in prison though to differing degrees.

Maqdisi's detachment from other prison inmates had deepened during the months in al Jafr.

As the day of his release approached, he talked about returning to his family, and his writing, about expanding his audience throughout the Muslim world, while taking care to avoid the kind of offence that could land him back in prison.

Zarqawi, on the other hand, was torn between two families: the one in Zarqa, and the one he gained in jail. His al Jafr brothers were a cadre of men devoted to him personally, and willing to follow him anywhere. With the amnesty, the survival of his family was suddenly in doubt.

The release of so many prisoners under amnesty meant a much lighter workload for the prison staff. Rumours were abuzz that the entire facility would be soon shut down for good.

Zarqawi had travelled to Amman, visited his mother in Zarqa, for a few hours, then turned around, and driven through the night in a friend's car to arrive at al Jafr before daybreak. Now here he was, back inside the outdoors of the hated prison, ministering to other inmates, like a field commander, checking the morale of his troops.

***

Six months after regaining his freedom, Abu Musab Al Zarqawi strode into the departure lounge of Amman's Queen Ali International Airport with a plan to escape Jordan for good.

He carried a freshly minted Jordanian passport no. Z393834, along with a Pakistani visa stamp, and a serviceable cover story: Zarqawi, the war veteran and ex-convict, was going into business as an international honey merchant.

He had thought to bring along his mother, the fifty-year-old Dallah-al-Khalayleh, a useful prop for someone trying to pass as a simple businessman, looking for partners for his apiarist venture. Notably absent were his wife and his three children. Zarqawi's true destination was no place for a young family, besides he had already planned for picking up a second wife, once he settled.

However, he had prepared for the reception the Mukhabarat, the Jordanian intelligence had prepared for him. As he approached the gate, several large men in dark suits grabbed Zarqawi by the shoulder and quickly hustled him into the side room, leaving his exasperated mother spluttering in the corridor.

Minutes later, he was sitting in the spy agency's headquarters, visibly struggling to contain his rage.

The man who sat opposite Zarqawi had by now interrogated the jihadist so many times that he could practically deliver his lines for him.

Abu Haytham, the intelligence service captain, then in his fifteenth year in the Mukhabarat's counter-terrorism division, had followed Zarqawi's preparations for weeks and arranged a pre-departure chat.

He had never been impressed by Zarqawi, regarding him as another hothead, louder and more aggressive than most, but lacking in the kinds of intellectual, or organisational talents that might make him exceptionally dangerous.

Zarqawi had been right about one thing: he had committed no criminal offence, at least nothing of a magnitude that would warrant a dramatic scene in front of his mother, and the scores of airport passengers. But, the Mukhabarat was not about to let him slink away easily. His prison stint had only hardened his views and expanded his network of possible co-conspirators. And now, he had a plane ticket to Peshawar, Pakistan, gateway to the Hindu Kush Mountains and, just beyond then, Afghanistan. Osama Bin Laden was living in Afghanistan by then. The Saudi extremist had blown up two US embassies in Africa in 1998, and declared a war on the United States.

The captain had not yet divine Zarqawi's true plans, but he was certain, they had nothing to do with raising honey bees in Pakistan's northwest mountains.

Legally, the Mukhabarat could detain Zarqawi for days, as they searched his belongings that quizzed his relatives and associates. The spy service could hold him as much as they wanted to.

Zarqawi, still, straining to keep his anger in check, as he waited in the spy agency's interrogation cell, knew this as well as anyone.

In the past, Zarqawi had not always been so pliant with Mukhabarat. Its first encounter with the man then known as Ahmad Fadil al Khalayleh, was an adrenaline-infused struggle, and very nearly proved fatal.

On March 1994, Mukhabarat raided an apartment where Zarqawi was staying. At that time, the intelligence service was rolling up a cell of Afghan war veterans connected to what appeared to be a serious extremist plot. Members of this cell, tied to Abu Muhammad al Maqdisi, had acquired land mines and anti-tank rockets and were preparing to attack Israeli soldiers at one of the border crossings with Jordan. A known leader of the cell was Zarqawi, then a twenty-seven-year-old Afghan veteran, who worked as a video store clerk, and spent his free time meeting secretly with small groups of Islamic radicals.

As other cell members disappeared into the Mukhabarat prison, Zarqawi moved from his house to the apartment to plan to flee Jordan. He was finalising his escape plan, just as Mukhabarat's officers gathered in an alley behind the building to prepare for the assault.

The agents watched the apartment throughout the day to see when Zarqawi would come home, and then waited for hours after the lights went out. At 1:00 a.m., using a key secured by the landlord, they quickly slid back and began creeping the stairs. They found Zarqawi alone in the backroom, dead asleep.

A wall of men fell on top of Zarqawi and struggled to pin him, while another in the raiding party snatched the weapon.

He lunged instinctively and tackled a man, an Egyptian who, fortunately, for the officers, had not been armed.

The officers then tossed the pistol, an M15 automatic, with three loaded clips, into their van along with the cursing suspects. Zarqawi still ready to kill, sat glaring at the agents from the backseat, with his matted hair, and torn nightshirt, tattoos poking out below the sleeve. He was angry, screaming curses, and called them *kafirs*.

In the Mukhabarat's fortress-like headquarters, senior officers watched their men, working in a small, glaringly lit cell, trying to wear the suspect down. Zarqawi was having none of it. He looked and sounded like others, but with an aggressiveness, that reminded the officers of a caged animal.

In fact, Mukhabarat knew a lot about Zarqawi even in those early days before prison. Between his thick police file, and the spy agency's legions of informants, the officers were quickly able to fill the gaps.

Ahmad Fadil al Khalayleh, as the records showed, had been troubled since childhood, taking the hard path, from vandalism to drugs, and alcohol, to more serious crimes.

He was born October 30, 1966, to parents of working-class Jordanians: a civil servant father who worked for Zarqa's municipal government, and a devoutly religious mother who adored the young boy above his seven sisters and two brothers. The family lived in a modest two-storey house perched on a hill, above a large cemetery where

Zarqa's working class buries its dead.

The graveyard is in shambles, with a few thousand crumblings, and hand-lettered tombstones strewn across a slope, filled with countless weeds and feral cats.

It is also the closest thing in the neighbourhood to a public park. The boy who would become Abu Musab al- Zarqawi spent countless hours playing in the cemetery as a child. Later as a youth, the graves would become the backdrop for his first forays into law breaking.

His ancestors came from a large and respectable East Bank tribe, the Bani Hassans, a biographical fact that normally carried certain advantages for a young man looking to make connections and find work in a patriarchal society like Jordan.

However, Zarqawi had blown one opportunity after another. He dropped out of high school, despite above-average grades, and test scores, showing an aptitude for art. He went into two years of compulsory military service but then got into a city job his father had arranged for him.

His criminal career began at age twelve. He had cut a neighbourhood boy in a street fight and then progressed into pimping, drug dealing, and assault. By his late teens, he had acquired tattoos, and a reputation as a heavy drinker, and street tough who took pleasure in brutalising his victims, and opponents with fists or blades. Security officials and acquaintances, who knew him at the time, believed that he forced himself on younger men, with the idea of sexual conquest.

He was twenty-one when he married his younger cousin,

Intisar, who quickly bore him a daughter. But Zarqawi's great love remained for his mother. Dallah al Khalayleh fretted over her troubled son, but she never stopped believing in his basic goodness or gave up her certitude.

She also understood her son's intellectual limitations. Years later, when journalists would show up at her house, to ask about Zarqawi's reported accomplishments as a commander and a bomb maker, she would be genuinely amused.

In fact, it was her mother who nudged Zarqawi into joining the Islamists. She signed him up for religious classes at the local al-Husayn Ben Ali Mosque, hoping that he would find better role models among the imams and the pious youth, with their theological debates and fund-raising drives, to benefit Muslim holy warriors in Afghanistan.

To everyone's surprise, Zarqawi plunged into Islam with all the passion he had reserved for his criminal pursuits. He swore off drinking and became a regular at Koran discussions and Friday prayers. He devoted propaganda videos and audiocassettes to the sectarian wars being fought in Afghanistan, Bosnia, and Chechnya.

And when the prayer leader at the local mosque asked for volunteers to fight against the communist oppressors of Afghanistan's Muslims, Zarqawi's hand went up.

He arrived at the Afghanistan-Pakistan frontier in the spring of 1989, weeks after the last Soviet troops withdrew, but just in time to join the Islamist assault on the pro-Moscow Afghan government that was left to fend for itself after the Russians pulled out.

One of the Afghan veterans who greeted him at the airport would later remember a wiry young man, who seemed eager, but also oddly self-conscious.

He said little, explaining at one point that he was embarrassed to speak, fearing he would betray his inadequate schooling and thin grasp of the Koran. Although it was already hot, he insisted on wearing long sleeves to cover up his tattoos.

Zarqawi's first assignment was to write articles for a jihadist magazine describing *mujahideen* exploits, on the battlefield, a job that proved taxing for a young man of limited schooling. Among his first friends were Saleh al Hami, a fellow journalist who had lost his leg to a land mine.

Zarqawi spent long hours at the man's bedside as he discovered, becoming so impressed with the devotion that he arranged to have one of his sisters flown to Pakistan to marry the man.

His brother-in-law would later move to Jordan's admiring biographer, Al-Hami remembered Zarqawi as highly emotional, and quick to cry whenever he read the Koran. Most of the Arab fighters tried to avoid such displays, but not the Jordanians.

During breaks in training, Zarqawi wandered around the Pakistani city, sometimes visiting a local mosque that had become a favourite for Arab fighters. Years later, the mosque *imam* still vividly remembered the earnest young Jordanian who seemed preoccupied with his past sins.

Zarqawi's first taste of combat came in 1991, when *mujahideen* rebels launched an offensive against government-held towns, in Afghanistan's eastern provinces of Paktia and Khost. Zarqawi fought with enthusiasm, and quickly gained a reputation for bravely bordering on fool hardliners, comrades remembered.

Once, according to Azzam, he single-handedly held off a column of a dozen, or more Afghan government troops, during fighting in the eastern city of Gardez, allowing time for others in his unit to escape.

He would never be a martyr, but in the mountains of eastern Afghanistan, he earned his credentials as a *mujahid* – a holy warrior.

By the time he left Afghanistan in 1993, he was a combat veteran with a few years of battlefield experience. He had been steeped in the doctrine of militant Islam learning at the feet of radical Afghan and Arab clerics who would later ally themselves with the Taliban or with Osama Bin Laden.

He had gained formal military training at a camp operated by Abdul Rasul Sayyaf, the Afghan rebel commander who would also mentor Khalid Sheikh Muhammad, the mastermind of September 11, 2001, attacks on Washington and New York.

Like the other Afghan fighters, he had also drunk from the heady cocktail of battlefield camaraderie and the rebel's impossible success. A ragtag army of Afghans and Islamist volunteers had defeated the Soviet superpower.

In 1993, Abu Musab al-Zarqawi and hundreds of other Jordanian veterans returned home to a country they barely knew.

However, it was only Jordan that had changed. In four years, while Amman and other big towns had grown larger and more modern, Zarqawi and his comrades had travelled backwards in time, journeying to Taliban-controlled Afghanistan, a place by every measure lagged centuries behind the rest of the world.

Now back in his hometown, Zarqawi had become his self-chosen nickname – 'the Stranger.' Even a trip to the local market was a reminder of the gulf between moderate easy-going Jordanian, and the strict Islamic disciple Zarqawi had witnessed in Afghanistan.

He complained to friends about immodestly dressed Jordanian women and the mixing of unmarried couples at cafes and cinemas.

He grumbled about pornography vendors, and liquor stores, which, years earlier, he patronised.

Even his own family disappointed him: his mother and sisters refused to wear the burka-styled veil, commonly worn by Afghan women, and his brothers allowed their families to watch un-Islamic movies and comedies on TV. The news shows that Zarqawi occasionally watched were even more upsetting, bringing reports of progress, by both the Palestinians and the Jordanian monarchy in negotiating treaties with Israel.

The very idea of peace with a Jewish state was an abomination to many Islamists. Some formerly steadfast supporters of King Hussein never forgave the monarch for this act, Zarqawi would take a stab at a normal life, spending his days renting out Hollywood movies, and Islamist propaganda tapes at the video store.

But inevitably, he was drawn toward the one thing that had given him a purpose.

He read books about early Islamic videos and became particularly fascinated with Nur ad Din Zengi, a warrior prince who ruled Damascus in the twelfth century.

Nur ad-Din had famously destroyed a European Crusader army and sought to unify a patchwork of Muslim kingdoms under a single sultanate extending from southern Turkey to the Nile River.

After his soldiers killed the French-born prince of Antioch, Nur ad-Din arranged for the sovereign's head to be placed in a silver box and sent to the caliph in Baghdad as a gift.

Years later, Zarqawi came to view himself as a modern incarnation of Nur ad Din and would seek to emulate his military strategy. But for now, Zarqawi was prepared to start small. He tracked down an old acquaintance from Afghanistan, the preacher and scholar named Abu Muhammad al Maqdisi, showing up at his house in Amman to say that he wanted to work 'on behalf of Jordan', as Maqdisi later recalled.

The two began a year-long partnership that began with Koranic study groups, for other Afghan veterans and progressed to the organising of small cells for more ambitious endeavours.

Maqdisi would write later about his early days with Zarqawi, as young men rallied around their calls and circulated their books and messages.

Similar groups, also led by disaffected ex-*mujahideen*

fighters were forming simultaneously across Jordan, and some carried minor attacks against liquor stores, and other symbols of Western vice.

Soon, Zarqawi, too, was pushing to do something more dramatic than photocopying religious tracts.

He suggested ways to disrupt upcoming parliamentary elections in Jordan, talking excitedly about possible targets until others in the group became nervous. He wanted everything to be done quickly and wanted to achieve all his ambitions in a matter of months, if not hours.

By early 1994, the group had a name: *Bayat al Imam,* or the Oath of Allegiance to the Prayer Leader. They also had a small stock of weapons from an unauthorised source.

Maqdisi, who had lived in Kuwait, at the time of the 1990 invasion by Saddam Hussein's army, had acquired a few mines, grenades and artillery rockets, left behind after Iraq retreated in 1991, and hid them in his household furniture when he moved to Jordan after the war.

The spark that significantly propelled the group into action came on February 25, 1994, when a Jewish extremist opened fire on praying Muslims in a religious shrine in the West Bank town of Hebron, killing twenty-nine men, and boys and wounding scores of others.

Incensed by the murders, the group decided with Maqdisi's reluctant support, to use their weapons in a coordinated attack on an Israeli outpost along the border.

The plan called for striking the guard station with back-to-back suicide bombers followed by small-arms fire.

The plotters never had a chance. The Jordanian intelligence, with its vast network of informants, inevitably learned the plan and moved quickly to squash it.

Its senior officers launched raids, ending the dramatic arrest of Zarqawi in his bed on March 29. He and twelve other members of the cell eventually signed confessions admitting to possessing illegal weapons and plotting an act of terrorism. Although, the extremists believed that their penalties only strengthened their faith in the religion.

After Zarqawi and Maqdisi both drew prison for fifteen years, the greater likelihood was that the men and their movement had been silenced for good. And if Jordan's prisons could not control them, the Mukhabarat had a variety of alternate methods that could deliver the same result.

The truth was, the leaders of the Mukhabarat were not entirely sure what to do with Zarqawi when he suddenly emerged from the prison in the spring of 1999.
The spy agency was still pondering the question six months later, right up to the morning he turned up at the airport with his mother and a pair of coach class tickets for Pakistan.

As Zarqawi was taken into custody for three days, they found a handwritten letter in one of the bags and pored over every line for possible coded messages, eventually concluding that it was a harmless greeting from one of Zarqawi's friends to a mutual acquaintance in Pakistan.

Intelligence officers tried quizzing Zarqawi directly, asking the same question in different ways. The detainee freely admitted that he hoped eventually to settle in Pakistan, finally, as his honey business was doing well enough to support a family.

His discomfort became hardly surprising. For one thing, he missed prison.

Harsh though it was, al-Jafr had given Zarqawi an identity and a community. Life outside just left him feeling anxious and disoriented.

To keep Zarqawi off balance, the Mukhabarat employed a strategy of regular harassing visits to Khalayleh home at odd hours, even late at night, and ask Zarqawi to take a ride with them.

Invariably they would end up at headquarters for chats that often went for hours. A key part of the things would be a recitation of things the agency's informants had overheard Zarqawi say or do, just to remind their guest of how closely he was being watched.

He had no choice but to submit amidst a tag team of interrogators and techniques, without handcuffs or restraints, maintaining his usual icy indifference in a sparsely furnished office.

When the subject turned to religion, Zarqawi became animated.

He seemed to enjoy showing off his knowledge of the Koran and the Hadith, the collection of apocryphal sayings of Muhammad and his companions, extensively mined by jihadists to justify their beliefs including killing non-Muslims and apostates.

Though Zarqawi talked like a religious radical, the agency's intensive surveillance showed that his behaviour was filled with contradictions and carried echoes of his religious past.

He would disappear for hours to the home of a Zarqa woman who was not his wife, and then he would head directly to an Islamist gathering or a local mosque for evening prayers. The intelligence officers believed that he would habitually lie about the most insignificant things, and he would stick to the false story even after being confronted with contrary evidence.

His behaviour was so baffling that Jordanian intelligence officials hired psychiatrists to review his files and make an assessment.

Though inconclusive, their review suggested that Zarqawi could suffer from a kind of multiple personality disorder, one in which the subject's deep insecurities and shattering guilt battled with an outsized ego convinced of its greatness.

Some of his Islamist friends also noticed his strange demeanour. One recalled that Zarqawi would sometimes sit for hours in a favourite falafel shop in Zarqa in his Afghan garb, without speaking to anyone.

Zarqawi would soon leave with his mother for a Pakistan-bound flight. There was no interference this time, but Jordanian officials would still be watching.

***

On 30 November 1999, Jordanian investigators were running a wiretap on a twice-jailed Islamist militant when an ominous phrase turned up in one of the daily transcripts stating that the time for training was over.

The suspicious call came from a phone in Afghanistan, and the speaker gave a kind of coded instruction.

Over the next two weeks, American counter-terrorism teams would arrive to assist the Jordanians in reconstructing what became known to history as the Millennium Plot, following a trail of clues across at least six countries. Organised by an al-Qaeda associate in Afghanistan, the Jordanian portion of the plan called for a wave of suicide bombings and small-arms attacks targeting not only Amman's Radisson, but also an Israeli border crossing, and a pair of Christian shrines, popular with Western tourists.

A separate plot to attack Los Angeles International Airport was foiled when a US customs agent arrested a bomber as he attempted to cross the US Canadian border, in a car packed with explosives.

Seized documents and an expanded surveillance web identified still more alleged participants, raising the number of suspects to twenty-eight.

Out of all names, one name evoked a surprise: a Jordanian from Zarqa whose given name was listed as Ahmad Fadil al Khalayleh. Zarqawi was back.

When he left Jordan, Abu Musab al Zarqawi had made it as far as western Pakistan and then appeared to have gotten stuck.

The informant who briefly trailed him sent back word that he was attending daily prayers at an Arabic-speaking mosque in Peshawar and staying clean. Now, just weeks later, he had resurfaced with a bit part as a consultant to one of the biggest extremist plots against Jordan in years.

Zarqawi had only played a minor advisory role, but wiretaps that linked him to the plot were sufficient to earn him new criminal charges, and a guilty verdict in absentia. He would be also featured in a report that landed at the CIA's Amman station.

In dismantling the plot, the Jordanians saved lives while averting an economic and political disaster.

The jihadists had deliberately targeted symbols of Jordan's vital tourist industry, at a moment when the country and its unexpected young monarch were still finding their footing after King Hussein's death.

Nine months into his reign, Abdullah II was struggling to implement economic and political reforms in the face of heavy resistance from Jordan's old guard, including the army generals, security chiefs, and tribal leaders who had held positions of privilege under his father. A successful attack could have altered the face of Jordan, crippled its economy, and weakened the new king's grip on the country.

The Islamists had signalled their determination to attack Jordan, and they had come close to succeeding.

And even though some of the participants were now in jail, the key planners were in Afghanistan, where they were free to try again. Among this group was Zarqawi, whose intentions were now clear. In September, Zarqawi had sat in the Jordanian intelligence office, begging for a chance to put Jordan behind him and start a new life. Less than three months later, the spy service was bitterly ruing the decision to allow him to leave.

The Jordanian intelligence would soon learn about

other plots to attack the country. The next one to invoke Zarqawi's name would be organised and planned by him alone.

Zarqawi's sojourn to Pakistan had not gone as planned. He arrived in Peshawar in September to travel onward to the northern Caucasus, where a new war pitting Chechen separatists and Islamists against the Russian Federation were just getting underway.

If he could link up with Chechnya's volunteer Islamic International Brigade, Zarqawi would at least have a chance to fight Russians, something he had never managed to do during the Afghan civil war.

But it was not to be. Pakistan's government, which helped bankroll the Afghan rebels in the 1980s, was less tolerant of itinerant Arab jihadists, in 1999, and Zarqawi struggled to obtain connections and travel documents.

As he waited, most of the Islamist army in Chechnya was destroyed when Russian planes dropped massive fuel-air bombs into mountain passes on the Chechen-Dagestan border.

Then, six months, onto his trip, Pakistani officials notified him that his visa had expired, and he would have to leave the country. Zarqawi was either confronted with a choice of either returning to Jordan-with the near certainty of arrest and imprisonment for his role in the Millennium Plot-or heading across the mountains into Afghanistan, a decision that offered far less appeal than it did when he last visited.

Not only had the country been devastated, by six years of civil war, but the conflict's newest phase also lacked the moral clarity, that had attracted Zarqawi and tens of thousands of Arab volunteers, in the 1980s and 1990s.

Now, instead of a struggle between Islamists and communists, the Afghan contest pitted a confusing array of Muslim warlords and Taliban generals against one another in ever-shifting alliances.

Still, Zarqawi chose Afghanistan. With a pair of friends, he made his way to Kandahar, eventually arriving at the headquarters of the one former Afghan Arab who might have been expected to welcome him: Osama Bin Laden. But instead of getting a warm welcome from his old *mujahideen* comrade, Zarqawi was rudely snubbed.

The al Qaeda founder refused even to see Zarqawi, instead sending one of his aides to check out the Jordanians

Bin Laden's caution with visitors of any stripe was likely well-founded: the deadly attacks on two US embassies in Africa, the previous year, had landed Bin Laden on the FBI's most wanted list. Bin Laden had a good reason to be wary of visitors who associated themselves with Muhammad al-Maqdisi, Zarqawi's former cellmate, and mentor.

Maqdisi had infuriated the rulers of Bin Laden's native Saudi Arabia with his essays calling for the violent overthrow of apostate Saudi regimes. Bin Laden had problems with Saudi leaders, and publicly associating with Maqdisi would make things worse.

Zarqawi was left to languish in a guesthouse for two weeks, before Bin Laden finally dispatched a senior deputy, a former Egyptian army officer named Sayf al-Adel, to meet with him.

Al-Adel, writing about the events, years later, acknowledged that he also was leery of Zarqawi, a man who already had a reputation for being stubborn and combative.

After exchanging traditional greetings and hugs, al-Adel took of the moment to size up the Jordanian. It was not an encouraging first impression.

Zarqawi's trustworthiness remained in question, so al-Adel proposed an experiment: Let the Jordanian run his training camp, specifically catering to Islamist volunteers from Jordan and the other countries of the Levant as well as Iraq and Turkey.

Al Qaeda would provide the startup money, and then watch from a distance to see what Zarqawi would accomplish.

The distance, in this case, would be some three hundred and fifty miles: the camp for Levantine fighters would be somewhat remote, al- Adel acknowledged, located near the Iranian border in Herat, a city on the opposite end of Afghanistan from al-Qaeda's base. Zarqawi would not be obliged to swear allegiance to Bin Laden, or to sign on to every point of al-Qaeda's ideology. But there would be plenty of cash from Gulf patrons, as well as what al-Adel described as full coordination and cooperation to achieve our joint objectives.

His first training base was initially made up of only a handful of close friends from Jordan, along with their families. But Zarqawi sent invitations to some of his old *mujahideen* comrades and prison contracts, and soon others were making the trek to western Afghanistan.

When al-Adel stopped for weeks later to check on

Zarqawi's progress, he counted eighteen men, women, and children.

In another two months, the camp's population had swollen to forty-two people, including Syrians and Europeans.

One of the Syrians, Abu al-Ghadiya, a trained dentist and comrade from Zarqawi's *mujahideen* days who spoke four languages, served as a kind of travel agent and logistics chief, in a preview of a role he would presume later when he ran the Zarqawi network's pipeline through Syria and into Iraq.

For a moment though, the most reliable route for recruits headed for Afghanistan passed through Iran. Although Zarqawi disliked Shiite Muslims and viewed Iran's leaders as heretics, he managed to link up with several helpful Iranians who ran safe houses and smuggled men and supplies to the Afghan border.

According to al- Adel, Zarqawi was kept in the dark about al-Qaeda's plans until after the strikes in New York, and Washington was carried out. But, Zarqawi's Herat base would be targeted by the Americans along with Bin Laden's in the weeks of fighting that followed.

Zarqawi's disciples and their families eventually organised a convoy of vehicles and travelled across Afghanistan to join al-Qaeda in the defence for Kandahar.

The US-backed Northern Alliance, supported by American commandos and air strikes, had already captured Kabul, the capital, and was preparing to march on the Taliban government's final stronghold.

But soon after the Herat group arrived in Kandahar, a

US bomber struck a house where senior al-Qaeda leaders were meeting, wounding several of them and burying others, including Zarqawi, under debris.

The Jordanian was pulled from the rubble with serious wounds, including several broken ribs.

He was still undergoing treatment when Bin Laden fled, deserting the Taliban and stealing away to his private sanctuary in the eastern mountains, the fortress known as Tora Bora.

Zarqawi collected his followers and a few al-Qaeda stragglers and dashed in the opposite direction, toward Iran, where he sought safety in the border towns through which his recruitment network once ran. There the refugees huddled in small groups, as al-Adel recounted later, to consider their dwindling options. In eastern Afghanistan, Bin Laden's mountain redoubt had fallen under heavy US bombardment. In Iran, government officials who had initially granted entry to the al-Qaeda refugees, including most of the Herat contingent. Where could al- Qaeda's men find a haven that offered both physical safety and a chance for the organisation's surviving members to rest and regroup?

In Iraq's northeastern mountains, there was one such place. Just a few miles from the Iranian border, a handful of Kurdish villages and towns had attained a precarious autonomy outside the writ of Iraqi dictatorship.

Beyond these charms, northern Iraq offered other advantages for a Jordanian on the run. Zarqawi could blend more easily with the local population than he did in Afghanistan, where he spoke none of the languages.

And, the region's extreme isolation offered a chance to recuperate without interference.

After reaching the Ansar al-Islam base, Zarqawi moved into primitive quarters in the tiny village of Sargat, a cluster of stone hovels on a dead-end road leading up into the hills.

The main base in Sargat consisted of seven small buildings, without heat or electricity, except for a single generator, encircled by earthen walls and bunkers festooned with black banners. A separate cluster of cinder rock dwellings served as housing facilities for Zarqawi's men, who mostly avoided blending with their Kurdish-speaking counterparts.

With a handful of his Herat followers and a few thousand dollars of leftover al-Qaeda money, he set about recreating the training camp he had established in Afghanistan.

There would be important differences, starting with this absence this time, of any significant al-Qaeda influence now that Bin Laden was hiding more than two thousand miles away. He could have new allies and supporters, including sympathetic Islamists in Baghdad, who sheltered him when he travelled there in secret to obtain medical treatment for his broken ribs.

Until 2001, Zarqawi's two great hatreds were Israel and the government of his own country Jordan. Now the pain of his broken ribs provided a constant reminder of his wish to inflict harm on the United States.

Zarqawi's tough character had been thrice remoulded: by prison, by war, and by the responsibilities of command at the helm of his Afghan training camp. He had come to regard himself both as a leader and as a man with a destiny. And now, in al-Adel's view, his energy and thinking had been altered again, honed this time by hatred and enmity against the Americans.

In conversations with disheartened Islamists in the bleak months of 2002, he talked of the epic conflict still to come, and how he had been steered by destiny to precisely the right place for engaging the great enemy of Allah, according to Fuad Husayn, a Jordanian journalist, who met Zarqawi in prison and later penned a biography about the leader's early years.

Zarqawi was left free to build his network without fear of attack or interference. CIA officials at the time understood that the Jordanian was becoming increasingly dangerous.

He became busy training his recruits at the Ansar al Islam base while dispatching envoys to Middle Eastern and European capitals, seeking money, volunteer, and allies.

He was able to forge ties between Algerians, Moroccans, Pakistanis, Libyans, and other Arab extremists located throughout Europe. Also, he managed to connect militant cells in thirty countries.

***

The line of visa applicants outside the Jordanian Embassy was small for a Thursday, even one in scorching early August when temperatures routinely top one hundred degrees before 10:00 am.

Only a few dozen Iraqis had arrived midmorning on August 7, 2003, forming a queue that hugged the shade of a concrete wall that ran along the front of the building.

Dusty taxis and sedans rolled to the curb to discharge passengers as the Iraqi guards, their uniforms already stained with sweat, gestured and barked with more than the usual gusto, evidence of jitteriness that had infected the staff in the past twenty-four hours.

A day earlier, someone had tossed a handwritten note over the wall, warning that the compound was about to come under attack.

The embassy's security detail had taken the note seriously, yet they were mystified by the strange threat.

The kind of carnage that would soon become so familiar – the car bombs and suicide assailants that blew up outside mosques and marketplaces was still unknown in Baghdad.

And why would the embassy be singled out? Jordan after all was a brother Arab State that had deep historic and cultural ties with its Iraqi neighbour, and the embassy itself, a handsome two-storey villa in one of Baghdad's most fashionable districts, served mainly to assist Iraqi travellers.

Amman, so stable and so affordably close, had long been a preferred destination for middle-class families looking for a shopping holiday or simply an escape.

The high demand for visas was the main reason the Jordanians erected the embassy's high wall, built not for security but to control the daily crowds that had become as much a part of the scenery as the palm trees along Arbataash Street.

And so, the sudden appearance of a shabby green passenger van at the embassy's front gate stirred concern, but not panic. As the sentries watched, the young driver pulled to a spot within a few feet of the concrete barrier, then hoped out of the vehicle and began walking away from the embassy building at a fast clip.

In the seconds before the guards could make their way over to investigate, the bomb hidden inside the van's cargo was detonated by remote control.

The blast was so powerful it sent the van's front section spiralling skyward to land on a rooftop two buildings down.

It tore a thirty-foot hole in the embassy's barrier wall, killing guards and visa applicants and crumpling the frames of passing cars.

The explosion shook a nearby hospital so violently that some doctors thought that the hospital itself was under attack until the waves of wounded began flooding the emergency ward.

Seventeen bodies were recovered-all of them Iraqis, including entire families with children who were incinerated inside passing cars.

The severed head of a young girl, her long hair scorched and tangled, lay in the street, discovered by a passerby who covered it with cardboard and then, amid the horror and confusion, began frantically digging in the hard dirt to try to bury it.

For ordinary Iraqis, the killings of innocents outside the embassy reinforced a sense of abandonment, a feeling that the American occupier cared little about Iraqi self-governance and was unwilling or unable to provide basic security.

At 4:30 p.m. on August 19, 2003 – twelve days after the Jordanian Embassy bombing – Viera de Mello sat at his desk on the hotel's third floor, oblivious to the large flatbed truck racing its engine at the entrance to the same narrow alley that had until recently been blocked.

Two foreign visitors and a handful of UN aides had arrived in the diplomat's suite for a meeting on Iraq's refugee crises, and they had just finished introductions when an explosion sheered away the building's front side.

The truck's driver had detonated a monstrous bomb rigged from an old aircraft munitions, obliterating the vehicle and cleaving through three floors of UN offices like a knife through a layer cake.

The discovery of the young suicide bomber's body in the wreckage removed any doubt that the attack was the work of extremists and not, as some US officials initially suggested, an attempt to score-settling by loyalists to the former Iraqi regime.

Bush, in one of his first public statements on the bombing, acknowledged that al-Qaeda-type fighters appeared to be infiltrating the country.

 The next strike was worse than the others and occurred not in Baghdad but in Najaf, a Shiite provincial capital and home to one of the most important shrines for the country's majority Shiite Muslim population.

August 29, 2003, was a Friday, the Muslim holy day, and huge crowds had jammed the city's gold-domed Imam Ali Mosque to hear a sermon by Ayatollah Mohammad

Bakir al-Hakim, a highly influential Shiite cleric who had returned from exile in Iran in the weeks after the US invasion.

On this day, the portly cleric climbed up the mosque's minbar in his robe and turban to deliver a blunt critique of the occupational forces, decrying their failure to bring security to the country, and specifically mentioning the bombings at the Jordanian Embassy and UN headquarters.

Hakim had just finished his sermon and was walking toward his motorcade when a car bomb exploded, followed quickly by a second. The blasts killed at least eighty-five people who had crowded the plaza for a glimpse of the cleric and wounded more than five hundred.

Thousands of worshippers and pilgrims fled the shrine in a panic, trampling over the dying and injured as they rushed toward the gates. Of Hakim, a man who had embodied the hopes of so many Iraqis as weeks as Americans, nothing identifiable was found except for a hand bearing the imam's wedding ring.

The CIA officials at Langley believed that intercepted calls linked Zarqawi not only to Najaf carnage, but also the UN attack and perhaps the embassy bombing as well.

Somehow, just five months after the destruction of the Ansar–al Islam camp, Zarqawi had managed to move his network into a strange capital and build an operation with sufficient intelligence gathering, firepower and logistical support to carry out a chain of sophisticated, large-scale extremist attacks in close succession.

Zarqawi was not only part of the worsening violence in Iraq, but he was also helping direct it.

Captains and sergeants who once served Saddam Hussein now enlisted in Zarqawi's army, and some rose to leadership positions.

Others offered safe houses, intelligence, cash, and weapons, including investigators who later concluded about the aerial munitions and artillery shells that provided the explosive force for Zarqawi's biggest car bombs.

The insurgency was not only real, it was winning. In the eyes of ordinary Iraqis, they appeared to be powerful and largely unchallenged.

The disaffected Sunni Muslims and former officers of Saddam Hussein's security establishment had been handed a perfect opportunity to regroup.

The continued sense of isolation in the Sunni heartland, the complete dissolution of the army, and other institutions of security, rigid de-beatification, and the lack of economic opportunities, or political direction gave these regime elements the confidence they needed to repair their networks and re-establish themselves.

Zarqawi, after months of fighting, from the shadows, was gaining confidence as the de-facto leader of a full-blown insurgency in Iraq. His movement, now supported by thousands of embittered Iraqis, and sympathetic Islamists from across the Muslim world, would soon pose the greatest threat to American ambitions in Iraq.

For years afterwards, when CIA officials would dissect the mistakes of the war's early months, some would marvel at the improbable confluences that enabled Zarqawi to achieve so much so quickly.

In January 2004, some ten months after he arrived in Baghdad, Abu Musab al-Zarqawi sat at a keyboard to compose a letter to Osama Bin Laden. It had been two years since his departure from Afghanistan, and almost four years since the al-Qaeda founder had refused to meet him in person at his Kandahar compound. But now Zarqawi was ready to offer a truce.

A lot had happened since their last communication and Zarqawi felt compelled to account for his time in Iraq, as though Bin Laden had somehow missed the news of the insurgency.

The situation in Iraq was different from anything the two commanders had experienced in Afghanistan.

Zarqawi maintained that he was making good progress in the campaign he had started, and hoped that Bin Laden might be willing to help. But first, he would offer a jihadist's view of the battlefield and sketch of the major combatants, including his small army.

He started with the Americans, rebuking them in the latter. He was equally scornful of the minority Sunnis of Iraq. He dismissed Iraq's majority religion as worse than paganism, having nothing in common with Islam, except in the way that Jews have something in common with Christians under the banner of the People of the Book. Also, he believed that Shiites had designs on destroying the Sunni faith, and they had craftily allied themselves with the US occupiers.

His organisation, though small had been behind nearly all the major extremist attacks in Iraq, excluding the far northern cities, with twenty-five strikes in all.

But he could accomplish much more with al-Qaeda's official endorsement and global resources. If Bin Laden agreed with Zarqawi's strategy, he was prepared to swear allegiance.

Zarqawi, a foreigner, had managed to build such an impressive network after less than a year in the country. Clearly, the Jordanians were getting help from the Iraqis. But he also was displaying undeniable skill as an organiser and a strategist.

Zarqawi's intelligence-collection ability was remarkably effective, judging from his ability to strike many miles from his presumed base. His security showed surprising sophistication, including a knack for flying just below the American's electronic surveillance nets.

Operationally, he was audacious yet careful, picking relatively easy targets, and powerful but simple bomb designs. Most impressive of all, was his ability to think strategically.

Zarqawi was not merely seeking to wage war. He was changing the battlefield itself, using terrorism as a brutal force for creating new enemies and allies as it suited his purposes. Just now, it suited Zarqawi to stir hatred between Iraq's Sunnis and Shiites.

While Zarqawi hoped to create problems for Iraq's interim leadership and American occupiers, the sectarian violence he instigated quickly developed momentum.

Shiite self-defence militias, some of them just as vicious as Zarqawi's thugs, seized control of entire neighbourhoods and waged running duels with US troops as well as rival Sunnis. Some like the Badr Brigade, turned to Iran's security service.

Zarqawi had essentially created a three-sided war, with US forces drawing fire from the other two sides at once. His embrace of revolting violence, so passionately described in his letter to Bin Laden, had been synthesised in a book, titled 'Management of Savagery.'

Ever since Zarqawi arrived in central Iraq, armed with only a few weapons, some cash, and his ambitions. His stated goals were to isolate and harass the American occupiers and ignite conflict between Iraq's Shiite and Sunni communities. He had managed to achieve both, and what is more, Iraqis had come to blame the Americans for the violence that he had sparked.

As he had hoped, Iraq was sliding into chaos, and Zarqawi would soon unveil new tactics to deepen the misery in the country and horrify the Western world.

***

Zarqawi was an upstart who lacked formal education and had never been regarded as having the vision or brainpower to run a large organisation. He also lacked the kind of institutional support that had helped make Bin Laden successful, including backing from recognised Islamic scholars whose fatwas gave spiritual cover to such violent deeds as killing unarmed civilians or employing suicide tactics.

Zarqawi sought no such approvals, and he had taken upon himself the responsibility of deciding how jihad against US forces would be waged.

In 2004, the Iraqi city of Ramadi was not yet the capital of the Islamic state of Iraq, as Zarqawi's followers would soon call it. But already, in the early summer, there was little doubt about who controlled the town.

He was seen rarely in the town but his Iraqi deputies earned notoriety as colourful butchers.

Zarqawi celebrated his rise in the most wanted rankings with a video, posted to jihadist websites. In it, he was introduced under his new moniker – 'the sheikh of the slaughters' and his voice boomed with confidence.

He talked about famous Muslim warriors such as Musa Ibn Nusayr, a hero of the Islamist conquest of Spain, implying his place in the chain of great men.

Then he made an impassioned plea for Muslims from across Iraq and around the world to join him.

His intended audience by now knew exactly the kind of battle he meant. The Jordanian men carried out dozens of executions, many of them videotaped, including the beheadings of a Bulgarian truck driver, a South Korean translator, and an Egyptian contractor.

Scores of others would follow, including Americans, Britons, Japanese, Austrians, and Italians. Lebanese kidnapping victims who were freed through ransom told stories of torture and unimaginable cruelty in makeshift prison; of poor immigrant labourers who lacked money for ransom being killed slowly with electric drills; of other victims being held down while their tongues were hacked out.

Young foreign-born Islamists who answered Zarqawi's

call to jihad most often ended in suicide bomber school. Some would be called upon to sacrifice their own lives to destroy targets with no discernible gain other than to kill innocent Iraqis who happened to be in the wrong place. In recruiting volunteers for suicide bombings, Zarqawi was knowingly defying a Koranic commandment that strictly forbids Muslims from taking their own lives. Some Islamic scholars have held that military suicide missions might be permitted under extreme circumstances, and jihadists have argued for decades over exactly where the lines fall.

Zarqawi seized on a small loophole in Islamic law and stretched it to absurd proportions, using handpicked clerics to sanction the use of 'martyrdom operations' for any purpose that suited him.

The result was a torrent of suicide attacks unrivalled in the history of the jihadist movement, scholars later concluded.

In videotapes appealing to recruits, Zarqawi offered the usual platitudes about heavenly rewards. More appealing, perhaps, was his invitation to be part of a movement that transcended history itself.

The liberation of Muslim lands was a worthy goal, but it was only the start. Zarqawi promised nothing short of a reshaping of the global order.

For the first time, Zarqawi also revealed a conviction regarding his destiny as a midwife for the new golden age of Islam. He referred to apocalyptic passages in the Hadith describing the end-time struggle that would lead to Islam's ultimate triumph.

According to the ancient prophecies, mankind's final

battle would be fought in northern Syria, near a village called Dabiq. The story echoes early Christian teachings about the epic contest between forces of good and evil at Armageddon.

The claim was audacious. Around the world, other Islamist leaders and religious scholars argued furiously about Zarqawi.

Among his harshest critics were some fellow jihadists, some of who went Zarqawi well. One of the sharpest rebukes came from the leader's old cellmate and mentor from Jordan, the man who was first to recognise Zarqawi's leadership potential within al Jafr Prison.

Abu Muhammad al-Maqdisi had been in and out of detention during the years when Zarqawi was away, and the differences that emerged between the friends during their last weeks in jail had widened in the years since. Now Maqdisi watched in disapproval as his former protege killed Muslim men, women, and children who had nothing to do with overthrowing a corrupt leader.

A religious back clash with Zarqawism stirred among mainstream Muslims as well.

The most significant repudiation of Zarqawi's ideology came from his native country, organised by the man whose amnesty decree in 1999 had inadvertently given Zarqawi his chance.

Since his arrival in Iraq, Zarqawi had become a master at exploiting the contradictions in the system, surrounding himself with like-minded clerics, who issued fatwas to condone suicide bombings and the killing of Muslim innocents, actions that would be regarded as anti-Islamic under almost any reason able interpretation of Koranic texts.

Each bombing shown on the nightly news, each grotesque video uploaded to the Internet, brought Zarqawi closer to his goal. And until now, the rest of the Muslim world had offered nothing substantial in reply.

***

When an Iraqi detainee called Mubassir made a confession of eight pages of typed notes in front of seasoned interrogators, it was by far a remarkable revelation about Zarqawi that had entirely eluded the Americans until now.

The border towns along Iraq's western frontier were already considered Zarqawi country in the early months of 2006.

Zarqawi's criminal network and his reputation for personal advice inevitably had been drawing the attention of Jordanian spies who worked in border towns.

The officials soon came to know that the Jordanian had a spiritual advisor, an Iraqi imam called Sheikh Abd al-Rahman, who lived with his young family in Baghdad.

And the two met regularly, about once every week to ten days.

For Zarqawi's hunters, it was the biggest break since the search began nearly three years earlier. The doubts grew after the Americans checked out an address for a Sheikh al- Rahman in Baghdad and found a house in a predominantly Shiite area – certainty the last place anyone would expect to find a Zarqawi confidant.

US and Jordanian officials raced to gather whatever they could on Zarqawi's supposed father confessor. Drones hovered over the expensive house where the man known as Abd al Rahman lived and trailed his silver sedan when he rode around town with his chauffeur.

Undercover agents in traditional Arab clothes waited near his mosque to snap secret photos of the young cleric with the close-cropped hair and trim beard.

Finally, the images were shared with Jordanian intelligence's new star informant. It was widely known within extremist networks that Zarqawi had a young spiritual advisor, but the man was known only by a fake name, a nom de guerre. The cleric in the photographs was the same adviser. He was sure of it.

Now came the wait. For two weeks, airborne cameras watched the house and followed the silver sedan on its mundane trips to markets, schools, and social outings. Each morning, the chauffeur waited in front of the house, and each evening, the cleric and his family returned home.

At Balad Air Base, the analysts watched their video screens and wondered if something had gone wrong. Had Rahman been tipped off? Should they have simply arrested the cleric and tried to get him to talk?

Then, around noon on a stifling hot Wednesday – June 7, 2006 – CIA officials watched from their monitors as a sedan made a sudden break from its usual orbit.

It meandered through residential neighbourhoods and then turned to enter Baghdad's main freeway, heading to the northeast.

On the on-ramp, the car abruptly stopped. Rahman got out of the car and began speaking on his cell phone.

A few minutes later, a small blue truck pulled up behind the sedan, and Rahman climbed in.

It was a classic car swap, the kind used for decades by spies, to throw pursuers off the track.

The truck sped through Baghdad's outer suburbs and then headed north, away from the city, and into the open countryside.

Rahman was on the move and heading away from the capital. Some officials guessed towards Yusufiyah. But they were wrong. Instead, to their surprise, the car continued north for thirty miles, then veered east. Rahman's destination was now unmistakable: he was heading straight towards Baqubah, just as the Jordanian intelligence chief had predicted.

The vehicle's occupants made yet another attempt to shake off any pursuers.

Just inside Baqubah's city limits, the truck pulled into a parking lot where a different vehicle – a white pickup with a red stripe was waiting. Rahman got out to speak to the pickup's driver, then for the second time, in an hour, he switched vehicles. Soon, he and the white pickup were heading north again.

About three miles from town, outside a tiny village called Hibhib, the pickup turned onto a smaller dirt road lined with thick groves of palm trees and then proceeded down a driveway leading to a beige two-story house with a carport. The dwelling was all but obscured by a canopy of palms and dense shrubs, and it was protected at ground level by a wall and a metal gate. The Americans watched as the driver spoke to someone inside the compound, who opened the gate to let the truck inside.

Rahman climbed out of the passenger seat, and then the driver backed the vehicle down the driveway and drove away.

It was 4:55 pm., Baghdad time. Every eye in the operations centre was now fixed on the grainy image of the small house under the palms. CIA analysts and military operators in the room had been waiting nearly three years for such a moment.

The opinion was divided. Some officials believed that the person they were watching was none other than Zarqawi. Others thought that they were moments away from their biggest kill so far.

They soon watched a guy coming out in black who then meets Rahman and takes him to the house. Then, a consensus came that the person was none other than Zarqawi.

A team of Delta commandos was on standby in Baghdad. Forty miles away, and now the command came from them to board the chopper. To the construction of all, one of their helicopters was having engine trouble. Agonising minutes passed.

At that moment, two American F-16 fighter jets were on routine patrol over central Iraq, under a policy that required twenty-four-hour coverage in case US troops needed immediate support.

One of the jets was being refuelled and was effectively out of commission, but the other was redirected towards Baqubah. An air traffic controller read a set of co-ordinates, and the fighter was soon screaming toward tiny Hibhib, less than five minutes away.

The officials wanted to catch Zarqawi alive, and then the plan was put on second thoughts because they thought they could not wait. It was nearly 6:00 pm when the bomb was dropped by F-16 fighter jets.

The fighter had swooped over the house, but to the surprise of those watching the screens at Balad, the building did not explode.

The pilot made a second pass, this time releasing a GBU-12 Paveway, a five-hundred-pound guided bomb.

From the centre of the F-16's video screen came a brilliant flash followed by three jets of smoke, and dust, one shooting skyward, and the other billowing through the palm trees. About a hundred seconds later, a second bomb hit in the same spot.

It took the Delta team another twenty minutes to arrive by helicopter. The commandos raced up the driveway on foot, just in time to see Iraqi police loading a stretcher into an ambulance next to a rubble pile that had been Zarqawi's hideout.

The Iraqis backed away at the sight of heavily armed American commandos, and soon the soldiers were staring into the bloodied face on the stretcher. He wore a thin beard and dusty black clothes, and he was bleeding from a deep gash on his left cheek. If the soldiers looked closely, they might have noticed an odd scar on his right arm, the legacy of a long-ago surgery to remove the tattoo.

Gravely wounded but alive, Zarqawi opened his eyes to see a ring of American faces looking down at him. Startled, he mumbled something unintelligible and tried to roll off the stretcher to get away, only to be stopped by American hands, some of them tattooed.

Years later, some of the soldiers present at Hibhib would claim that the commandos delivered the final blow, squeezing the life out of Zarqawi, as he lay on the stretcher.

An autopsy found no evidence of it, concluding that Zarqawi had minutes to live in any case, his lungs and other internal organs having been crushed by the intense pressure wave from the exploding GBU-12 bomb.

A medic at the scene noted that Zarqawi's carotid artery had already collapsed from internal bleeding, and blood seeped from his nose, and ears as he wheezed through a few last breaths.

***

PAKISTAN, AFGHANISTAN AND BEYOND

Pakistan has been through terrible moments before but has never been placed in such as embarrassing position when it had to surrender its army to India, and the loss of East Pakistan. It left the country with great shame and anger. It has muddled through other wars and defeats at the hands of India, through devastating floods and earthquakes, and enormous political turmoil.

As Pakistani historian, Farzana Shaikh observes, 'Pakistan is no stranger to chaos. But what makes this moment in Pakistan's history exceptional is the threat it is seen to pose, simultaneously, to the security of its citizens, to the welfare of its regional neighbours, and the stability of the wider international community.'

According to the New York Times-based Committee to Protect Journalists, Pakistan became the most dangerous place in the world for journalists to work – not just because of the Taliban, but also because of the security agencies.

The war in Afghanistan has continued, but now Pakistan has been considered widely, the most fragile place in the world, because of what might happen there politically and because of what it can foster elsewhere.

It is the most unstable country and most vulnerable to extremist violence, political change, or economic collapse.

Its multiple long-term and short-term problems seem

insurmountable by the present military and civilian leadership. It is not yet a failed state, but it may become one, as its febrile state worsens.

It still has a powerful army and a corrupt and run-down but functioning bureaucracy, judiciary, and police force; its economy would be viable if its problems were properly addressed, and its population is hard working. Pakistanis perform outstandingly well in academia, the arts, television, fashion design, pop music, and of course cricket. However, they lack adequate services such as health care, full literacy, a modern educational system, population control programs, and real economic growth.

The civilian political elite has failed to give the country leadership. Holding virtually all the political and economic power, the elite lacks all sense of responsibility towards the public, refuses to pay taxes, and is immeasurably corrupt.

Whenever elections are held, invariably after a long bout of military rule, the political elite has failed to govern effectively. The development of an alternative democracy is stuck.

At the same time, a powerful military dictates the country's foreign policy, especially towards India, Afghanistan, and the United States, eats up over 30 per cent of the national budget and runs several unaccountable intelligence services.

For several decades, the army has used Islamic extremists to pursue its foreign policy agendas in India and Afghanistan, but that practice has backfired and, created an international extremist movement called the Pakistani Taliban.

The UN estimates that Pakistan's 185 million population will grow to 275 million by 2050. Despite its primarily agricultural economy, Pakistan can barely support its existing population, and it is difficult to see how water, food, land, and services will be available for 90 million more people. One-third of the Pakistanis today lack drinking water, another 77 million have unreliable food sources, and half the school-age children do not go to school.

The literacy rate is 57 per cent, the lowest in South Asia, and not better than the 52 per cent that prevailed at the creation of Pakistan in 1947. Half of the population is not even looking for jobs, since they know that they will not be able to find them.

The country needs at least a 9 per cent annual growth rate to employ it's under the twenties, who make up 60 per cent of the population.

The 37 per cent of Pakistanis who are under the age of fifteen give Pakistan one of the world's largest youth bulges. In an economy whose 2.6 per cent growth rate, on average, for many years, fails to provide them with jobs or food security, a never-ending stream of young men facing a future of little promise and are ready to sign on to jihad.

Pakistan's short-term problems are worsening daily, creating far-reaching regional and global problems. Since 2005, a Taliban insurgency has aimed to topple the government, defeat the army, and install an Islamic extremist state.

The Pakistani Taliban currently control large tracts of the northwest, and other extremist groups from around the country have joined them in destabilising major cities such as Karachi and controlling large tracts of southern Punjab.

Ethnically, the Afghan and the Pakistani Taliban movements are mostly tribal Pashtuns: Afghanistan has twelve million Pashtuns, but Pakistan has another 30 million. They are a constant source of manpower for fighting the Americans in Afghanistan, and the army in Pakistan.

A full-scale revolt is underway in the country's largest province, Baluchistan: the rebels are fighting the army and demanding separation from Pakistan. Both sides in the Baluchistan conflict are committing some of the worst atrocities in Pakistan has ever witnessed. In Karachi, with its 18 million people, in Sind province, and the Northern Areas, unattended ethnic inequality has led to an insurgency and acute ethnic conflict.

Intolerance is growing, and minority religious groups such as Christians and Hindus, who have lived peacefully with the majority of Sunni Muslims for decades, are now fleeing the country.

Muslims from other minority sects – Shias, Ahmadis, Ismailis, and others – are being visibly targeted, and those who can afford to are settling abroad.

After years of low revenue collection, failure to develop new industries and trading partners, joblessness, and chronic inflation, the economy has been collapsing.

Acute shortages of gas, electricity, and water have led to the closure of the industry. Pakistanis had carefully watched the 2011 Arab Spring, but many feared that such a movement in Pakistan to destabilize or remove the existing regime would lead not to greater democracy, but a revolution led by Islamic extremists.

As far as the United States is concerned, Pakistan should be the keystone country in the region, but after 2001, two American administrations virtually ignored its worsening domestic crises, as long as Pakistan kept delivering some degree of cooperation in the US-led war in Afghanistan, which to the Bush administration meant one thing: that Pakistan capture members of al-Qaeda.

The Afghans, who have been at war since 1978, are exhausted. Most Afghans want US troops to leave, but are divided between wanting a peace settlement and wanting to share power with the Taliban. While the Pashtuns favour a total US withdrawal, and a deal with the Taliban, the non-Pashtuns in northern Afghanistan and many of the 5 million population of Kabul prefer to see the war continue until the Taliban are defeated. The new urban elite does not want to see the United States abandon Afghanistan, as the Soviets did after their withdrawal in 1989.

Many Afghans fear that once the West leaves, their country will plunge back into civil war.

Stabilising Afghanistan and Pakistan and ensuring that Al Qaeda plays no role in either country has become even more vital in the aftermath of the revolutions sweeping through the Arab world in 2011.

The Arab Spring has given the heart of the Muslim world a real opportunity for faster economic progress, democracy, literacy, and stability. But it has also given Al Qaeda enormous opportunities to re-enter the Middle East and disrupt or co-opt the ongoing revolution process. The only organised political parties were the Islamists in countries such as Egypt, Tunisia, and Libya, where autocratic rules were overthrown through mass movements.

The fear was that Al Qaeda could return on the backs of these Islamist parties. A State failure in Pakistan or Afghanistan, unleashing a flood of extremists from these two countries, would quickly destabilise the Middle East and destroy the changes there. Instability in the Afghanistan-Pakistan region would also directly affect India and its ongoing war with domestic Islamic extremism.

The states of Central Asia – Tajikistan, Uzbekistan, Turkmenistan, and Kyrgyzstan – are particularly vulnerable because extremists from these countries, who have spent the past few decades hiding out in Pakistan, are now making their way through northern Afghanistan back to their homelands. The fragile and authoritarian states of Central Asia may well become the next battleground for Al Qaeda and militant Islam.

The US-NATO plan depends on making peace with the Taliban, leaving the self-sustaining Afghan government and army to take over the responsibilities of security and governance and development.

Regional stability is essential if Afghanistan is to survive. This optimistic plan does not reflect the deep pessimism felt on the ground in both Afghanistan and Pakistan, but it may succeed.

Since 2009, the United States has spent over 100 billion a year on the troop surge in Afghanistan, while in 2011 the US defence budget has reached a staggering $671 billion. Between 2001 and 2010, the United States spent a total of $444 billion in Afghanistan, including $25 billion each for economic development, and Afghan security forces.

Worse, the Taliban insurgency is more intense than ever, the Afghan government is weaker than ever, and Pakistan is more vulnerable and lacks a positive relationship with Washington.

The most pressing issue for the Americans was the network run by Jalaluddin Haqqani in eastern Afghanistan, which was allied to both the ISI (who guaranteed their sanctuary in North Waziristan by refusing to go after them) and Al-Qaeda (which provided the latest technology, training, and inspiration).

The Haqqani network had access to hundreds of suicide bombers from the most militant madrassas in FATA and had the singular ability to mount devastating suicide attacks in major Afghan cities.

Primarily the United States and NATO have failed to create an indigenous Afghan economy, that is not dependent on foreign aid, or employment on US bases and that gives people real jobs and incomes. When the American troops leave, tens of thousands of Afghan drivers, cooks, guards and clerks, will be out of a job, because they will have no place in the local economy.

After 9/11, President Bush declined to invest in rebuilding Afghan infrastructure, such as roads, dams, and water and power supplies. Consequently, real economic growth, including the creation of long-term jobs, has been extremely limited.

In 2011, only 6 per cent of Afghans received electricity. Kabul – the largest city, with 4 million people – received partial full-time electricity only in January 2009, via a 20-megawatt power line from Uzbekistan.

Richard Holbrooke, Obama's special representative for Afghanistan-Pakistan who unfortunately died on the job in December 2010, initiated a new program to improve the economy and invest in agriculture, but it needed time and better security.

If there is to be an effective transition toward self-government, then clearheaded, visionary Afghan leadership is needed.

As the endgame approaches, intense competition has developed among Afghanistan's six neighbours: Iran, Pakistan, China, Turkmenistan, Uzbekistan, and Tajikistan. These countries have a long and record of monumental interference in Afghanistan. Now, they seem to be preparing to move in once again, recruiting their proxies among the Afghan warlords and spreading money and influence in the country.

The neighbour most vital for any peaceful resolution in Afghanistan is Pakistan, which has its ambitions and interests in the country, which it feels must be fulfilled. Otherwise, Pakistan's military can become deal breakers, unless they are satisfied.

After 9/11, the military regime of President Pervez Musharraf provided sanctuary to all the defeated Taliban leaders. In 2003, the ISI helped the Taliban restart their insurgency in Afghanistan and provided them with supplies, training camps, and infrastructure, even as Musharraf kept the Bush administration on his side by capturing and killing members of Al Qaeda.

Tensions between the United States and the Pakistan military also escalated between 2010 and 2011.

For the army, the killing of Bin Laden was the humiliating last straw, and a deep chill set in, just when the two countries needed more than ever to work together.

***

Pakistan has a litany of problems, some of which involve the military. It refuses to acknowledge or end its covert support for the Afghan Taliban.

It drags its feet on seeking a settlement with India. The anti-state Pakistan Taliban is growing. The military refuses to handle politically the separatist insurgency that has erupted in the Baluchistan province. Extremism in the army's ranks and concerns about the safety of Pakistan's nuclear weapons cause international apprehension. The military leadership fears that its officers and soldiers are becoming more intensely anti-American and so more susceptible to extremist propaganda.

On the other hand, the civilian government and the political parties refuse to address a wave of extremist tolerance against minority groups, both non-Muslim and Muslim. They take no responsibility for providing services to the public while indulging in large-scale corruption. They allow an unprecedented economic meltdown to become worse by declining to carry out reforms or listen to international advice.

They fail to disarm militants or address the situation in Karachi, where ethnic and criminal bloodletting leaves scores of people to die every month. Pakistan faces diplomatic isolation, as its relations with all major countries except for China are soaring dramatically.

Devastating floods in 2010 and 2011 and an epidemic of dengue (malaria) fever in Punjab in 2011 were unavoidable, but government concern and aid delivery were inadequate. Pakistanis are becoming to fear the worst: international isolation, anarchy, civil war, and a coup by Islamic militants.

Four factors have prevented Pakistan from stabilising and becoming a coherent state. First, the political elite has failed to establish a coherent national identity capable of uniting the nation.

The military defines Pakistani national identity defensively, in terms of the country's vulnerability, as a national security state, with a permanent mistrust of India. The politicians, in power, have never seriously tried to challenge this isolating self-definition by offering alternative policies, such as promoting good neighbourliness, ending support for Islamic extremism, fostering economic development, and providing education.

The Pakistani Taliban for their part would define Pakistan in religious terms: they call for the establishment of a state based on Sharia, or Islamic law, and for a caliphate, a supranational entity that would dissolve Pakistan's borders, and aid and abet Islamic extremism, and Al-Qaeda. The extremists lack sufficient support to seize state power, but they have a proven ability to disrupt the state and foment anarchy.

By 2011, the Pakistani Taliban were a much more dangerous entity than even the Afghan Taliban.

The Pashtun tribesmen who made up the original core of

the Pakistani Taliban had been joined by militants from Punjab, Karachi, and other places that have been involved in the war in Kashmir.

They provided a sophisticated, educated, and urban edge to the war they now waged against Pakistan's security forces and civilians.

Second, all these groups had camps in FATA where they willingly trained foreigners, especially European Muslims from countries such as Britain, Germany, and Sweden; these students then returned home to become extremists.

Third, they were far more ideologically extreme than their Afghan brothers and could depend on a large pool of recruits as fighters and suicide bombers. By 2011, the main Afghan Taliban had expressed their desire to talk with the Kabul government and the Americans, but the Pakistani Taliban were still adamant about Pakistan's destruction.

The second factor dividing the country is Pakistan's national security paradigm. Is it to remain India centric- as determined by the military?

The long-running civilian-military rift that underlines these two views has contributed to the army's rule of Pakistan for nearly half the country's existence. Whenever the army feels that its control over national security is being challenged – usually amid a political constitutional economic crisis, when an incompetent and corrupt civilian government is at the helm – it invariably overthrows the government and imposes military rule. This has happened four times in Pakistan's history, and military rule has often lasted a decade or more.

In the military view, Pakistan is constantly threatened

by outside enemies, particularly India, but at times also Afghanistan, Iran, or the United States. To stand up to this perceived threatening environment, it maintains an army of 600,000 men, the seventh largest in the world.

Its total security forces number more than 1 million men, armed with nearly one hundred nuclear weapons. The military consumes between 25 and 30 per cent of the budget. It can secure those state resources because the political elite is supine and corrupt, parliament does not insist on accountability, and the army retains control of foreign policy, national security, and the nuclear arsenal. No enlightened military leaders have arisen to try to change this status quo, despite the spread of democracy, and the demise of authoritarian forms of government around the world.

Third, Pakistan has become an abnormal state that uses Islamic militants – jihadi groups, non-state actors – in addition to diplomacy and trade to pursue its defence and foreign policies. These non-state actors have deeply antagonised their neighbours, all of whom have, at one time or another felt their pressure.

After September 11, 2001, the army's policies did not change, even though the whole world was now deeply aware of the threat posed by Islamic extremist forces and was less than tolerant towards them.

The fourth factor perpetuating Pakistan's fragility is the inability of its ethnic groups to find a working political balance with one another, and the failure of Pakistan's political system, its parties, and its army to help them do so.

Punjab, the second largest province geographically,

contains 60 per cent of the country's population. Seventy per cent of the army and a large part of the bureaucracy are drawn from Punjab. Punjab is also the most ethnically homogeneous province, with most of its population being Punjabi. The Baluch, Sindhis, and Pashtuns have one time or another felt underprivileged and resentful of the Punjabis. Punjabis contain 60 per cent of the population, so all the other nationalities put together cannot equal Punjab's weight in determining economic or national policy. Moreover, the other three provinces – Baluchistan, Sind, and Khyber Pakhtunkhwa – are often at odds with one another over issues such as electricity and the distribution of water. For smaller provinces, Punjab also constitutes the centre of the state because it is from Punjab that is bulk of the army and the bureaucracy is recruited. As a result of Punjab's dominance, resentment from the smaller provinces has ebbed and flowed over the years. They have mounted everything from political resistance, and civil unrest to terrorism and separatist guerilla wars; the current insurgency in Baluchistan province is the fifth of its kind. Hence the absence of a shared national identity that transcends ethnicity, tribe, religion, and language is a lingering problem for Pakistan. If Pakistan were a trading hub and a regional crossroads, using all its territory, all its ethnic groups would have a stake in it.

The military and the political elite are both to blame for perpetuating the four factors, and for failing to forge Pakistani unity.

The major political parties are run as family dynasties rather than democratic institutions, and they have rarely offered modernising policies that would reform the economy or society; they have rarely tried to live up to their responsibilities to the people.

Meanwhile, the long bouts of military rule, in which politicians were jailed or exiled, have made it unthinkable for educated young people to enter politics. The politicians' failure has sustained the army's strong anti-civilian prejudice and more recently fuelled public antagonism toward politicians and the democratic system. Such conditions have only helped Islamic extremists present themselves as incorruptible, clean alternative rulers.

These internal conflicts within the country's elite have prevented the rulers from noticing major shifts and challenges in the global environment. They have allowed history to pass them by. With the result, Pakistan has missed all recent global developments.

India's boom could have accelerated a similar expansion in Pakistan if the two neighbours had better trade ties. But instead, globalisation passed Pakistan by.

Many educated Pakistanis had no idea of the dramatic economic changes being wrought on the world stage, as Pakistan continued to export its traditional raw materials like cotton and rice, fought its proxy wars in Kashmir and Afghanistan, and stagnated.

In the past twenty years, it had not developed a single new industry or cultivated a major new crop, even though it is an agricultural country.

Globalisation made it vital for Pakistan to spend money on education, upgrade the skills of its workforce, and invest in new industries. Instead, Musharraf fuelled a consumption-based economy that rested on personal and state debt.

Pakistan, by contrast, has undertaken no major economic

or social reforms since the early 1990s.

The ruling elite refuses to tax itself or to invest its wealth in modernising industry and agriculture; the state-run industries are bleeding the country; and the army refuses to cut its expenses, even as it has expanded its tax-free businesses and property empires.

Only 1.8 million people pay income tax, and farmers pay no income tax, even though they are the best off due to the rapid rise in food prices. Corruption is rampant, and social services, especially education remain abysmal because every year government's spending on health and education is cut as military expenses increase. Literacy is at a miserable 57 per cent, the lowest in South Asia. Neither the politicians nor the army has ever called for a massive literacy campaign.

For the past twenty years, the country has lived off IMF loan programs, which have never been fully completed or complied with because the various governments have refused to carry out the reforms demanded by the IMF.

Other countries provide large amounts of aid, but Pakistan has very little to show for it. Between 2001 and 2010, the United States gave a total of $20.5 billion. Germany, Britain, Japan, and other donors, along with the World Bank and the Asian Development Bank, provided about half again the sum.

Out of the US funding, $14.4 billion went to Pakistan Army for operations along the Afghan border, while only $6.1 billion was used as economic aid, and most of that ($4.8 billion) was for budgetary support. When Richard Holbrooke first visited Pakistan in 2009, Pakistanis admitted bluntly that they had nothing to show for all the

US aid – not a hospital, dam, or university.

The government and the military further exacerbate Pakistan's crisis-ridden state by constantly feeding the public a false narrative; that the United States, India, and Israel are conspiring to undermine Pakistan and ultimately dismember the country; that the reason for the increase in Islamic extremism in Pakistan is the US occupation of Afghanistan; that the United States and India are arming and funding the Pakistani Taliban to weaken Pakistan; that Osama Bin Laden was never killed in Abbottabad; that if the United States were to leave Afghanistan, terrorism and suicide bombings would cease, and everything would return to normal. Indian external intelligence RAW (Research and Analysis Wing) abetted by the CIA, is said to be funding separatists in Baluchistan, and Sind to carry out acts of terrorism, while India lays down deep roots in Afghanistan.

These lies and myths confuse the public and youth, prevail over the objective or rational analysis, and make it easier to spread conspiracy theories. The political, intellectual, and media elites have never challenged them in a sustained way – many journalists are on the government or ISI payroll or receive other benefits or privileges. Among most academics, too, intellectual standards and honesty have been sorely lacking, except for a few superb scholars, who refuse to compromise.

Government servants, especially those in the foreign and interior ministries, tend to be subservient to the army, and groupthink disallows any real debate over policy.

For ten years or more, Islamabad has denied that Al Qaeda, the Afghan Taliban, or the Haqqani network was ever based on its soil, even though most of their leaders have been captured or killed in Pakistan. In recent years, the military has admitted to the Americans that these groups are present in Pakistan because the army is also intent on getting negotiations going between these groups and the United States. But the army will never admit it in public.

The false narratives give excellent cover to the anti-Indian jihadist groups, such as Lashkar-e Toiba, that have been trained by the ISI, and that have a working relationship with Al Qaeda and the Taliban.

The Pakistani state does not merely protect these jihadist groups and allow them to recruit and train cadres and mobilise funds; it portrays them not as extremists, but as benign social workers.

After when LT mounted attacks in Mumbai in 2008, Pakistan held LT leaders under discreet house arrest for a few weeks, then freed them. This non-punishment infuriated the United States, India, and the international community.

The constantly tense military-civil relations dominate Pakistan's politics. Three of the country's four military dictators were forced out of power by a mass movement, and simultaneously a constitutional crisis, an economic depression, and an increase in ethnic separatism. Every time a military regime is brought down, Pakistanis have had to go back and reinvent the wheels of democracy.

After a decade of military rule, civilian governments have been invariably incompetent and corrupt, and only await their denouement at the hands of the next military coup.

No elected government has yet been able to fulfil its whole term mandate before being voted out of office through another election. Every military dictator, too, had been forced out, usually by his inability to get himself elected for a second term as a civilian rather than as a military president.

Briefly, the tribes in FATA had been particularly receptive to radicalisation because of their history of poverty, underdevelopment, and religious conviction, and their constant state of rebellion to protect their rights.

The influx in 2001 of Al Qaeda and the Afghan Taliban into this region had acted like an economic and religious engine, driving the process of radicalisation.

Tribal resistance to the army began in 2004. The militants turned back each attack; enough to produce army defeats and humiliating cease-fires. That further emboldened them. Army attempts to raise local militias to fight them were a failure. The militants abandoned their traditional tribal chiefs and elders, who usually supported the government, and killed more than one thousand of them. Tens of thousands of tribesmen fled FATA. By 2010, the militants controlled all of FATA.

In 2007, various militant tribal militias formed the Tehrik-e Taliban Pakistan (TTP); that same year militants openly confronted security forces at the siege of Red Mosque, in the heart of Islamabad.

The army was forced to storm the mosque complex, killing more than one hundred people. Those militants who survived escaped to FATA and became suicide bombers. In 2007, fifty-six suicide bombings killed 865 Pakistani security forces and civilians, compared to just six suicide attacks the previous year. The losses in 2007 exceeded the total losses for all years between 2001 and 2006. An internal civil war had begun.

By 2011, more than 35,000 people would be killed, including 3,500 security personnel.

The extremists have also repeatedly challenged the election, by creating mayhem on the streets. In the first ten weeks of 2008, seventeen suicide bombings killed nearly three hundred people and left the country reeling.

The Pakistani Taliban controlled main roads out of Peshawar, and besieged the city; only months later did the army regain control.

Kidnappings for ransom rose dramatically in KP and FATA, where Baituallah Mehsud executed twenty-eight members of a tribal peace group who had met with the Pakistani Taliban. The new government had no clear plan on how to deal with the escalating violence and left all decision-making to the army.

The war in FATA left 1.5 million people displaced, while the yearlong unrest created severe economic and energy crises, with a chronic shortage of gas, electricity, and fuel. Musharraf, a recipient of more than $10 billion in aid from the United States, had failed to build a single electricity generating station. Zardari set up the Friends of Pakistan forum to beg traditional donor countries for more money, but they refused to oblige until the government first carried out major economic reforms.

To stave off a default, the government signed an agreement with the IMF for a loan of $11.3 billion, promising to implement economic reforms. In the meanwhile, FATA was the main base for Al Qaeda and Western jihadis, who were coming there in ever-increasing numbers to receive training.

The Americans were deeply worried that the Pakistan Army was mounting all too few operations in FATA; that it was instead striking peace deals with militants who refrained from attacking Pakistani forces, but eagerly attacked US forces in Afghanistan; and that it refused to disturb the Haqqani network in North Waziristan.

Pakistan was now inescapably becoming an unstable state, a continuing supporter of the Afghan Taliban, even as the army went up against its homegrown Pakistani Taliban. The army had underestimated Obama's resolve to deal more harshly with Pakistan than Bush had ever done. Yet as Obama sent more troops and aid to Afghanistan, Americans started to ask why he was doing so when the real problem was in Pakistan.

***

At the heart of Pakistan's rapid decline, its worsening relations with the West and neighbouring countries, and its image as the centre of global terrorism has been the army's continued reliance on proxy jihadi forces. Some of the jihadis were ready to carry out the state's bidding, but others were just easily turned against the military. In the 1990s, their main target was Indian Kashmir, but when the Taliban emerged, Pakistani militants went to Kandahar to fight for them.

Pakistan's strategic location, which could have been a vital economic asset to the country, was now a liability, as it became the central hub for the US war in Afghanistan, and as jihadis from surrounding countries flocked there. Pakistan's new global identity was not a model of innovation or modernity but a refusal for multiple extremist groups.

A decade after 9/11, its failure to address the extremist threat culminated in the breakdown of relations with the United States and NATO.

The country had also first used proxy forces just after it gained independence in 1947, when it sent thousands of Pakistani Pashtun tribesmen to battle Indian forces in Kashmir, triggering the first India-Pakistan war. Sixty years later the grandchildren of those Pashtuns would be urged to kill Americans in Afghanistan.

In 1962, following India's defeat by China, the military regime of Gen. Ayub Khan secretly sent several thousand soldiers disguised as guerillas to stir up rebellion among the population in Indian Kashmir. Code-named Operation Gibraltar, the infiltration was a failure, but it led to a second all-out war between the two countries, which Pakistan lost.

In 1971, the army created similar proxy forces in East Pakistan (now Bangladesh) to help it subdue the separatist Bengali insurgency, which was backed by India.

These proxy forces, some Bengali, but mostly Urdu-speaking Biharis as well as cadres of the Jamaat-e-Islami, carried out several massacres. Pakistan's defeat by India and the loss of East Pakistan-half the country- created strong feelings of humiliation within the military, which encouraged it to continue using proxy forces as an effective tool to weaken India and achieve revenge.

The military was to further bankroll the Sikh insurgency in Indian Punjab and, over the years, several tribal uprisings in northeastern India. A vicious tit-for-tat ensued, as

India in turn funded and supported Baluch, Sindhi, and Pashtun separatists in the 1970s and later. Baluchistan has undergone five insurgencies. In the 1980s, India backed the pro-Soviet Communist regime in Kabul, which launched its extremist campaign in northwestern Pakistan to counter the presence of Afghan mujahedeen.

Also in the 1980s, the ISI made a bold move to exert distributive control over billions of dollars in arms supplies, and cash supplied by the CIA for the mujahedeen.

Up to 30,000 foreign jihadis came to fight alongside the mujahedeen, and many of them were to stay in Pakistan.

The military took enormous credit for the defeat and breakup of the Soviet Union. After 9/11, Pakistan believed it could carry on similarly with the Americans – help the CIA with Al Qaeda, but assert its sovereignty and carry on with its agenda in Kashmir and Afghanistan.

In 1989, the ISI used residue of US funds for Afghanistan to support a mass movement in Kashmir against India that would last a decade. Many of Pakistan's generals were to remain influenced by the expansionist foreign policy, and the use of jihadis cultivated by Zia ul Haq, who took the country literally from one jihad to the next, without a break. Several Pakistani militant groups such as Harkat-ul- Jihad-al-Islami (founded in 1984) and Lashkar-e-Taiba (founded in 1982) were born in the crucible of the anti-Soviet Afghan war, before moving on to greater exploits in the 1990s.

At home, there was a rapid growth of madrassas, weaponisation, drugs, and crime, making these groups self-sufficient, as ISI funding for extremist groups was reduced.

As long as the Indian giant remained cowed and pro-Pakistan forces were successful in Afghanistan, no Pakistani government came up with plans to de-radicalise the militants and undertake educational and economic reforms.

Pakistan began to lose control of these groups in 1997 when the Taliban leader Mullah Muhammad Omar handed over all training camps for foreigners in Afghanistan to Osama bin Laden. In these camps, Kashmiri and Pakistani extremists mixed with young militants from all over the Muslim world, and from Europe, just as an earlier generation had done in the 1980s, in Afghanistan. Al-Qaeda's indoctrination had an enormous impact on them: some embraced the idea of global jihad, joined Al-Qaeda, and went on to provide it with skills and facilities. Both before, and after 9/11, all Pakistani insurgent groups used Afghanistan as an arena for virtual battle experience, increasing their militancy, raising their numbers, and sharpening their skills. These Pakistani groups would later turn against the regime in Islamabad and flourish as the Pakistani Taliban.

After the defeat of the Taliban, after 9/11 in Afghanistan, Musharraf and the military began the long process, overseen by the Americans, of capturing and killing Arab Al Qaeda members who had fled to Pakistan.

The United States gave cash rewards to Pakistani security officials, who had been involved in actions to kill and capture members of Al Qaeda.

A tiny minority of Pakistani officers from the ISI and Pakistan's special forces had jihadist sympathies, and disagreed with this policy; they left the army and joined militant groups.

The ISI also helped the Taliban raise funds in the Arabian Gulf States, and facilitated their acquisition of guns and ammunition. It set up training camps manned by its officers in Baluchistan province, where many Taliban leaders had settled. It set up a secret organisation to run the Taliban, even as it was cooperating with the CIA in apprehending Al Qaeda. Retired army and ISI officers, operating outside the traditional military structures, manned the secret organisation. For several years, the United States failed to detect this support base or understand how it operated. The main Taliban under Mullah Omar set up offices in Quetta and Peshawar; its leaders in Quetta directed the insurgency in southern Afghanistan. Another Afghan Taliban ally, Gulbuddin Hekmatyar's Hezb-i-Islami party, operated out of northern Pakistan.

From their bases in Pakistan, the Taliban launched two attacks into Afghanistan, while recruiting Pakistani Pashtuns to provide them with base security and additional manpower, even as they radicalised them for their cause. Thus, were born the Pakistani Taliban in FATA. They were local Pakistani Pashtun tribesmen who became radicalised after spending years in the company of either Al-Qaeda or the Afghan Taliban and receiving generous payments for services rendered.

Throughout this period, the veteran Afghan Anti-Soviet fighter Jalaluddin Haqqani played a crucial role in the army, creating temporary ceasefires, or bringing Pakistani Taliban to talks with the military.

In 2004, India and Pakistan also agreed to a ceasefire, alongside the disputed Line of Control, the border that divided Indian Kashmir from Pakistani Kashmir.

Significantly, that ceasefire has held ever since, even though both countries still maintain large numbers of troops on the border. As a result, young Punjabi militants from parties that had once fought in Kashmir became frustrated, split away from their mother parties, and came to FATA to fight for the Afghan Taliban. The tribal agencies were soon littered with camps of Punjabi militants who had received Haqqani's permission to set up shop.

The ISI soon lost control over these groups, which killed and bombed their way through Pakistan's cities, targeting specifically the offices of the ISI and other intelligence agencies. Only Lashkar-e-Taiba, by now the largest, best disciplined, and most highly trained extremist party, with some support in the army itself – remained loyal to the state, and sought to fight only India. But even LT leaders came under pressure from their cadres to fight the Americans, and so by 2009, its leaders allowed a limited number of young fighters to play a role in Afghanistan.

Over the next few years, FATA was to turn into a battleground, but the army remained extremely selective about whom it went after.

It hunts down only those who oppose the Pakistani state; it allows Afghan Taliban such as Jalaluddin Haqanni, who remains loyal to Pakistan, to thrive in North Waziristsan. Likewise, it leaves alone Pakistani Taliban commanders – such as Hafiz Gul Bahadur and Maulvi Nazir Nazir from South Waziristan.

The Pakistani State also used drones. The CIA ran the Pakistani air base at Shamsi in Baluchistan province, so some of the drones that killed militants in FATA took off from Pakistani soil. The drones have become the target of widespread public anger at the government, the army, and the Americans.

Drone strikes began in June 2004, and during the Bush administration (which ended in January 2009), a total of only forty-four were fired.

However, Obama saw them as a strategic rather than a tactical weapon and had authorised four times, as many, or one strike every four days. Pakistani critics maintained that while drones kill militants, they also killed hundreds of civilians.

Even in Washington, the CIA's authority over the drones has left the State Department out on a limb, because while State may have been pursuing talks with the Taliban, the CIA was bombing them.

In 2010, as violence by the Taliban intensified in both countries, more Pakistanis were asking why the military had pursued a policy of subterfuge with its people for so many years.

Soon after the Mumbai attacks, the Pakistani media became increasingly anti-American, depicting Pakistan's sacrifices in the war on terror and the lack of US appreciation for them.

Pakistanis began to compare India with Israel, which could do no wrong in American eyes, and Pakistan with the Palestinians, to whom the Americans always gave short shrift.

In July 2011, a string of high-level US visitors to India, and US and Indian companies investing in each other's territory, culminated when Secretary of State Clinton asked India to play a larger role in the region.

America's newfound love for India was loathsome for Pakistan, but Pakistan's military and political leaders never explained to the public that things had changed, that Pakistan could no longer have a relationship with the United States as a hedge against Indian power, and that Pakistan needed to repair its relations with India, which was streaming ahead of it in every week.

Fears about security inside Pakistan's nuclear facilities also started to become constant. At least seventy thousand people worked in Pakistan's nuclear industry, including security personnel. Anyone of them could become susceptible to extremist propaganda. After 9/11, the United States gave Pakistan more than $100 million to secretly bolster the security and fail-safe mechanisms around its bombs.

By 2010, Pakistan had more than one hundred nuclear weapons, a second-strike capability, and miniature bombs that it could place on long-range mobile missiles. But the army was still not satisfied that this was a sufficient deterrent against India and wanted more.

Nobody knows how much Pakistan spends on the nuclear program, because it is a state secret, and is presumably hidden in other budget lines like pension and health.

Meanwhile, Pakistan is the only country that opposes the proposed international Fissile Material Cut off treaty, which can cap fissile material stockpiles – a key Obama foreign policy aim. Pakistan says India has access to fissile material through its civilian nuclear program, so Pakistan will have to keep producing and stockpiling fissile material until it is satisfied enough.

As Taliban attacks became more audacious and widespread in Pakistan, concerns arose about the safety of Pakistan's nuclear components. Bombs were separated from their triggers and other components were stored separately.

Also, for quite a while, the army's lack of counterinsurgency training had proved devastating enough whenever it had been deployed in FATA.

In August 2008, for example, the generals sent the army to the Bajaur tribal agency, in FATA to rid it of Pakistani Taliban, promising a two-week campaign, but eight months later the army was fighting.

Counterinsurgency has a doctrine of 'clear, hold, and build' that is aimed at protecting the people and their homes. In Bajaur, the army's tactics were the direct opposite: it moved out the population, flattened villages with artillery, and used bombing and bulldozers to create vast free-fire zones.

Without a local population to provide them with intelligence, information or protection, the troops became sitting ducks for the rebels.

Some four thousand people fled Bajaur and became refugees, creating an enormous humanitarian crisis, but the army refused to allow NGOs to come and help. Among those who fled were tribal elders, and educated youth – all vehemently anti-Taliban – who had been protected, and would have provided the necessary backup to military operations. Getting counter-insurgency right is about getting the strategic priorities right; for some years the military still perceived India and not the Taliban as the greater threat.

In FATA, Taliban militants appeared to learn more quickly than the army. The Pashtun Taliban began to copy lessons from the LT's campaigns in Kashmir. Suicide bombing had never existed in South Asia before 1990, but when Tamil rebels introduced it in Sri Lanka, the LT in Kashmir and other groups quickly followed an example.

The LT called them 'fedayeen attacks' – rather than committing suicide with bomb-laden vests, militants would attack an Indian outpost to fight to the death.

The Haqqani network and Pakistan's Taliban commanders soon developed suicide bombing into a veritable industry, persuading, or forcing gullible Pakistani and Afghan teenagers to become bombers and then selling them to commanders in the field. Manufacturing parts of suicide vests became a cottage industry in FATA, with different families and villages producing the belts, ball bearings, and detonators while the Taliban provided the explosives.

Suicide attacks have now become a major tactic for both Afghan and Pakistani Taliban. In 2010, a total of eighty-seven suicide attacks in Pakistan killed more than three thousand people.

Pakistani generals seem oblivious to the fact that ending the Taliban insurgency in their country ad helping stabilise Afghanistan should be a higher priority than countering the Indian threat. They seem heedless of the fact that they need to end their policy of supporting certain Taliban while fighting others and instead start decentralising militant groups in Punjab, or that they need to end Haqqani's control over North Waziristan and push the Afghan Taliban into a dialogue with Kabul to end the war.

They seem to be unaware that their present course is

putting Pakistan's security in the hands of the Taliban; that the isolationist path is at odds with the army's strategic interests as well as those of Afghanistan, the entire region, and the West; and that it will ultimately endanger Pakistan's internal security and future development.

***

Due to institutional inertia, Bush had rarely reevaluated US strategic priorities in the region, his administration's ideological moorings saw the world in black and white – Iraq and Al Qaeda were the main threat, Afghanistan was an afterthought, Iran was an enemy, and Pakistan was an ally. Karzai kept raising with him the danger posed by Taliban resurgence, but to no avail, meanwhile, Pakistan saw Bush's inattention as a free pass to continue to support the Taliban while keeping pressure on Al Qaeda.

Until 2004, the United States had only 15,000 troops based in Afghanistan, which has a population, which has a population of over 30 million.

In 2007, as the Taliban insurgency was spreading, there were still only 25,000 US troops there.

Frustrated US officials in Pakistan believed that Washington did no serious intelligence gathering on the Taliban threat until 2006. Neither the White House nor the Pentagon was interested in monitoring Quetta or the Baluchistan-Afghanistan border, from which the Taliban infiltrated.

In the summer of 2008, the Taliban launched an offensive that, in June, killed more Western troops – forty-three – than in any month since 2001.

The Taliban's use of improvised explosive devices (IEDs)

increased by 200 per cent.

They undertook audacious attacks inside Kabul, and in Kandahar, a brilliantly planned jailbreak freed eleven hundred Taliban prisoners.

As a result of the deteriorating situation in the provinces, some thirty-six Afghan and Western aid workers were killed in 2008, and another ninety-two were kidnapped. Forty per cent of the country was now off limits to the UN and aid workers, while many Afghans and the international community held Karzai's government in low esteem for failing to tackle corruption or improve governance.

But all this was temporarily forgotten on a cold day in Washington when Obama took office. That day, the Taliban mounted three attacks in eastern Afghanistan, including a double suicide bombing that killed 15 people. In the south it was announced 650 schools were closed because of Taliban attacks, cutting off 200,000 children from education. There were not enough troops to guard everyone.

The United States had 161,000 troops in Iraq but only 32,000 in Afghanistan (along with 29,000 NATO troops).

Even as Obama urged European governments to send more troops to Afghanistan, polls showed that three-quarters of European voters rejected that idea. International patience with the war was waning fast. In 2008, the death toll for US soldiers in Iraq was down by one-third, but 151 died in Afghanistan, up from 111 in the previous year.

The UN said that Afghan civilian deaths increased by 40 per cent in 2008.

The reviews of the situation in Afghanistan that Bush had ordered up were now awaiting Obama's attention.

On January 21, 2009, Obama appointed veteran diplomat and peacemaker Richard Holbrooke as his special envoy for both Afghanistan and Pakistan (which would now be called AfPak).

Holbrooke put together a large interagency team and brought in academic experts so he could deal comprehensively with everything from military issues to economic aid, boosting education, and media spin.

The debate on how many troops to send to Afghanistan (detailed in Bob Woodward's *Obama Wars)* preoccupied the White House for months. Tragically, the near-exclusive focus on military engagement prevented greater discussion of important strategic issues. Afghanistan's economic, political, and social future; peace talks with the Taliban; and US, policy toward Pakistan. Holbrooke's office issued paper after paper on these larger issues, but they were rarely discussed.

Finally, the White House and the Pentagon agreed that 17,000 soldiers and 4,000 trainers would be deployed as soon as possible.

The first 8,000 soldiers – Marines- would go to Helmand province in the south, where the violence was worst; the south was the centre for insurgents, the main heroin production area, and the principal area of access to Pakistan and Taliban supply lines. Eight thousand British troops that had been deployed there since 2006 were too thinly stretched out, and had failed to establish peace.

Helmand had only 1 per cent of the total Afghan

population. According to the new counterinsurgency strategy that Petraeus favoured and that was being practised in Iraq, US forces should have been deployed in densely populated areas.

Soon, Obama had announced his plan to send an additional 21,000 troops to Afghanistan. His goal was to disrupt, dismantle and defeat al Qaeda in Pakistan and Afghanistan, and to prevent their return to either country in the future.

He doubled the number of civilian advisers and experts and increased funds for economic development and for building up the Afghan Army and police (but refused to define it all as nation-building).

He got tough on corruption within the Afghan government. For Pakistan, he had harsh words: he demanded that it do more to root out extremism but imposed few sanctions – and dangled few carrots – to enforce the threat.

Also, the Afghan 2004 presidential and 2005 parliamentary elections had been successful, with large voter turnouts, considerable public enthusiasm, and a wide choice of candidates. But in 2009 – when the country faced a full-blown insurgency and had a barely functional administration, economy, and army, and could ill afford an election – such a debate never took place.

The problem was that for the Americans, elections had become a litmus test determining everything else.

A US intervention in any third-world country now consisted of holding an early election so that the country would be dubbed as a democracy, and then the United States could head for an exit. By contrast, the European philosophy favoured the UN, which was to first build governance and economic infrastructure – nation-building – so that elections could be both meaningful and sustainable.

In 2009, the country had no party system, scant respect for parliament, and no public mobilisation, or electoral awareness campaigns, while the elected officials of the provincial councils, which should have been greatly empowered, had been ignored.

Instead, the patronage alliances made by warlords and powerful candidates continued to dominate the political scene, as they had in 2004. But in 2009, for very different reasons, the Americans and Karzai wanted elections and argued that any further delay would signal the weakness to the Taliban.

Meanwhile, throughout the summer of 2009, the Taliban were on the offensive, intent on disrupting the election. In the first six months of that year, their attacks had soared by 60 per cent over 2008.

In a single week in June, Taliban attacks had killed 250 civilians and soldiers in twenty-five provinces out of thirty-four provinces. It was the widest, deepest, and Taliban offensive so far, and their control had expanded to nearly half of Afghanistan's 364 districts.

The critical battlegrounds were the two provinces of Kandahar and Helmand, which had large Pashtun populations. In the 1990s, the Taliban (most of whom were Pashtun) had butchered many non-Pashtuns in the north and west, but now the north was relatively peaceful.

Back then in 2004, the UN had control over the election,

but this time around, Karzai had demanded that the UN hand over control to the Afghan-run Independent Election Committee (IEC), which was beholden to Karzai, as he appointed its members.

The international community's big great mistake was to agree to this demand. Some UN and US diplomats warned of massive rigging but were not listened to. Within a day of the election, Karzai's aides were claiming outright victory, while Abdullah Abdullah, who was believed to have won the right to a run-off election, pointed out the fraud and painted a bleak picture if the West did not recognise it.

Unfortunately, the international community conducted no post-mortem on the election, so when the parliamentary election came around a year later, nothing had been learned or rectified, and no plan was made to deal with Karzai's determination to overrule the elections' institutional mechanisms.

The IEC had asserted itself but left behind an intractable problem. Due to renewed Taliban threats, turnout among the Pashtuns was very low, because of which the Pashtuns lost 20 per cent of their seats to ethnic minorities, especially the Tajiks and the Hazaras in provinces where ethnic groups were mixed.

In 2010, Karzai felt trapped and was seriously considering declaring the elections invalid, which would have created an even bigger crisis.
He delayed the opening of the parliament, fearing a non-Pashtun majority that would reject any peace deal with the Taliban, amend the constitution to change from a presidential system to a parliamentary system, and reduce Karzai's powers.

The standoff continued till January 20, 2011, when the UN, the United States, and the European Union jointly expressed deep concern at Karzai's failure to open parliament and threatened that if the delay continued, they could not justify their expenditures on Afghanistan. Karzai finally backed down and opened parliament – four months after the elections had taken place.

Ultimately, a kind of solution was found. The IEC dismissed nine members of parliament on account of fraud and replaced them with another nine who were acceptable to Karzai, but more than half of parliament refused to accept the new members.

The lack of fair elections, the inequitable distribution of seats among ethnic groups, the war, and the continued economic deprivation have only intensified Afghanistan's long-running and unresolved ethnic problems. The divisions between the Pashtuns and the non-Pashtun nationalities that make up the complex weave of the Afghan national carpet remain deeply entrenched. The corruption and incompetence of the Karzai administration are still seen to benefit the Pashtuns.

US counterinsurgency and development spending had focused heavily on the Pashtun provinces where the Taliban insurgency was strongest, to the neglect of those dominated by ethnic minorities in the north and west. Non-Pashtuns remain furious that an estimated 70 per cent of all development funds are being spent in just two provinces in the south – Helmand and Kandahar.

Meanwhile, the talks between the Karzai government and the Taliban had galvanised non-Pashtuns to mount a fierce resistance led by the Tajiks, who oppose the secret talks with the Taliban and are unwilling to share power with them – the Taliban butchered them less than a decade ago, and helped Al Qaeda murder their leader, Ahmad Shah Massoud.

A strong grassroots movement had emerged among the non-Pashtuns that is critical of both Karzai and the Taliban. Left largely to their own devices, the Tajik, Uzbek, Hazara, and Turkoman minorities have achieved some successes (which stirs anger and resentment among the Pashtuns).

The non-Pashtuns who dominate the north and west have also linked up with the neighbouring states to open road and trade networks, import electricity and gas, develop mineral extraction, and create other profitable businesses.

Those benefitting are Iran and the Central Asian States of Tajikistan, Uzbekistan, and Turkmenistan. Herat, in the northwest, has forged links with Iran that have turned it into the country's most prosperous province.

The Pashtuns in the south and the east, by contrast, are stuck with their powerful neighbour Pakistan, which supports the Taliban with money and arms, but has done little to encourage trade or development, provide aid, or improve Afghan Pashtun lives. Pakistan, mired in its poverty, and deficient in energy and water, has had little to offer the Pashtuns.

Some Tajik and Uzbek warlords in the north had become so rich and powerful that they barely listened to Karzai. Governors, there have created their fiefdoms and maintained their militias that the NATO forces based there did not touch.

***

The Obama formula for Afghanistan failed to do several things: encourage Pakistan to change its policy of harbouring the Taliban, build up an indigenous Afghan economy, start talks with the Taliban parallel to the military surge, and persuade Karzai to improve governance and end corruption.

Lacking a reliable political partner in either Kabul or Islamabad, Obama was more dependent on the US military for his policy's outcome. Obama's greatest success – using funds made available by Congress – was to rapidly build the Afghan security forces to 350,000 men, but whether these undertrained and illiterate Afghan forces could not hold the country together once the Americans left was always debatable. Wars cannot be won through military means alone, especially when the occupying forces are trying to exit the country amid an insurgency.

Obama had been utterly trapped by the Bush legacy of failures in Afghanistan between 2001 and 2008, and by the power and authority of the US military establishment after September 11: it became arbiter, driver, and decider of US foreign policy. Obama's cold sense of reality could not free itself from the Pentagon's way of thinking or doing.

Despite Obama's overarching commitments to Afghanistan, the US military read his program to mean just one thing: more troops, which had been unobtainable while the Iraq war was at its height. Such was the expectancy of a rapid increase in US troops that bases were being built even before the troop numbers had been agreed upon.

Holbrooke opposed the troop buildup and pushed for resolving the Pakistan conundrum, negotiating with the

Taliban, and helping Afghanistan and Pakistan with their economies. Unlike the military, he did not see defeating the Taliban as an option. The White House snubbed Holbrooke, even though his views were somewhat like those of Obama's advisers.

But they hated him, and Holbrooke could never get a one-on-one meeting with the president. Some advisers even tried to get him sacked. In the deliberating situation, Obama seemed to exercise no authority over his staff. On December 11, 2010, Holbrooke collapsed in Clinton's office with a split aorta and died two days later.

US allies around the world asked what degree of personal commitment the president had toward Afghanistan. For a decade, the country had been one of America's biggest foreign policy challenges.

For all his misplaced ideological moorings, Bush had understood this when it came to protecting and projecting his wars. He cultivated common touch, constantly meeting Afghans – students, women, teachers, journalists, filmmakers, or members of parliament – hosting them at the White House and asking them about their problems.

Undoubtedly, Karzai presented an enormous problem for Obama. Once the darling of the West and a moderate, reasonable leader who seemed to have a good chance of taking Afghanistan out of thirty years of war, Karzai had lost way. He had been in power and isolated in the presidency for too long.

Over the decade, the few US and international officials whom Karzai had trusted moved on, leaving the Afghan president alone with his conspiracy theories. During the 2009 presidential election, he was convinced that the

Americans wanted to get rid of him, even as he stubbornly refused to correct his failures: corruption in the top ranks of his government and family and his lack of vision. He frequently told top US officials that of the three main enemies he faced – the United States, the international community, and the Taliban – he would side first with the Taliban.

After 2001, Western leaders had pledged never to abandon Afghanistan, but their commitments of money and manpower never matched their rhetoric. Sufficient funds to rebuild the country's infrastructure and economy never arrived, and the United States refused to deploy troops outside Kabul after the 2001 invasion, instead rearming over Karzai objection – the warlords who ruled the provinces like medieval barons.

Other complaints were also growing louder. Washington was failing to help provide electricity, build roads, and rehabilitate 3 million returning refugees.

The Commission on Wartime Contracting in Iraq and Afghanistan, set up by Congress in 2008 reported the waste and fraud $30 billion worth of contracts in the two countries, all of which had undermined US diplomacy, fostered corruption, and tarnished American image abroad. The United States had deployed more than 260,000 contracts, or the same number as US troops, to both countries. Karzai had repeatedly pointed out to Bush Pakistan's clandestine support of the Taliban.

Obama arrived in the office giving no sign of wanting to have a personal relationship with Karzai. He cancelled the videoconferences and issued a laundry list of issues that Karzai had to address: nepotism and corruption in the Afghan government, lack of good governance, and proliferating drug trade. He feared that Obama was out to replace him and so began to fear his political survival. Karzai was full of conspiracy theories about the Americans. According to one of them, the reason the United States would not deal decisively with Pakistan was that it was in league with Pakistan to weaken Afghanistan.

Karzai was his own worst enemy. He had refused to address any of the demanding issues that engulfed his administration. He failed to accept corruption was a core problem for the country and his people. He showed little interest in improving governance and capacity in his ministries. He rarely visited the army or the bureaucracy in training. He could not say no to his brothers, who fleeced the banks and were involved in multiple property acquisitions.

In Washington, the real debate was not over Karzai, but over whether to conduct a counterinsurgency campaign (which could require tens of thousands of troops) or a counter-terrorism campaign (which would involve fewer troops but rely on drones, missiles, and surveillance to take out extremists).

In 2009 and again in 2010, the military won out on obtaining more troops to do counterinsurgency. Based on the maxim, 'clear, hold and build,' and transfer to the Afghan insurgency was meant to be people-centric – winning over Afghan peasants, protecting them from the Taliban, and rebuilding their lives.

While carrying out counterinsurgency, the US military was also secretly conducting counter-terrorism, which then Vice President Biden had advocated. US Special Operations Forces carried out night raids, killing or capturing hundreds of Taliban commanders and fighters, but civilians were also inadvertently trying. The CIA's drone strikes in Afghanistan and Pakistan's tribal areas were also part of this secret counter-terrorism war, and they caused even more civilian casualties, which ultimately increased anti-Americanism in both countries.

McCrystal's shocking report made it easier for the Pentagon to ask Obama for more troops. But the White House was bewildered because it thought it had already provided the necessary number of troops – it had dispatched just four months earlier. The generals were now loudly talking about the aim of defeating the Taliban rather than disrupting and degrading them. This was far from Obama's original mission statement back then. The military seemed once again to be boxing Obama into a corner and taking control of the narrative.

The military wanted Obama to consider only three: dispatching 10,000 trainers, sending 40,000 troops, or sending 85,000 troops.

Once again, there was little discussion of Afghanistan's strategic political issues, such as its growing political and ethnic divisions, its economy, relations with Karzai, or the readiness of the Taliban for talks.

Pakistan occupied a lot of discussions but yielded few political answers. Instead, Leon Panetta, the director of the CIA, presented a list of clandestine counter-terrorism operations that the CIA wanted to conduct in Pakistan, such as stepping up drone attacks, raising the number of CIA agents and covert contractors, and even setting up a parallel intelligence organisation that would be hidden from the ISI.

Both the Pakistani and the Afghan governments resented

the fact that a major US escalation of troops was being undertaken without consulting them, or soliciting their views.

However, in November 2009, Obama announced his decision to enact the surge. He said that he would send 30,000 more troops but would start to bring them back in July 2001, when a transition to Afghan forces would begin.

At the United Nations, Obama's surge resulted in greater hostility from members. In January 2010, Kai Eide, the UN special representative for Afghanistan, presented a devastating report to the UN Security Council in which he said that the US emphasis on security over social and development issues would doom any efforts to stabilise the country. The central government was being weakened, he said, as 80 per cent of all aid was financed directly by Western governments rather than by Kabul.

Eide, whose term in Kabul lasted from 2008 to 2010, was a deeply honest and forthright individual who told the Americans and Karzai the truth. He made it clear that the Americans had never consulted with the UN, or with NATO about critical strategy-related questions, while the Afghan authorities had mostly been spectators, as the United States formed policy for their country. He was one of the first high-level officials convinced of the need for reconciliation with the Taliban, at a time when the idea was deeply unpopular. And, as with Holbrooke, the Obama administration chose to ignore his messages.

As the result, the first target of the US surge was Marjah, a small farming region in Helmand province. In mid-January 2010, the Marines began an offensive to clear Marjah. It was not a populous region (it had a population of just eight thousand people); nor was it of vital strategic importance. Most Afghans had never heard of it.

Helmand had a population of only 1.4 million people or just one-thirtieth of Afghanistan's total, but it was a base for the heroin industry, from which the Taliban profited, as well as a major route for supplies and recruits from Pakistan. The Taliban had ruled unopposed since 1993. After their defeat in 2001, they remained in control of Helmand, due to a lack of Western forces being deployed in the province. Finally, in 2006, 8,000 British troops were deployed in Helmand and heavy fighting broke out with the Taliban. The US Marine Corps eventually decided to move its forces to Helmand from Iraq, and the Marines had an independent command and decision-making structure within the US military.

Marjah was more about the Marines showing what they could do than it was part of a strategically defined offensive. Marjah had some strategic value, but because of the paucity of population, it could not be seen as part of counterinsurgency, which should have focused on the most densely populated areas. The Marines carried out a spectacular assault, using dozens of helicopters, and then immediately got bogged down as dug-in Taliban, suicide bombers, and mines took their toll. Three months later, the 15,000 troops were still unable to secure the region.

A total of $19 million in aid money was earmarked for development in Marjah, but only $1.5 million was spent. The Americans issued vouchers to farmers that would get them free seed and fertiliser, but the farmer rejected them because they feared Taliban reprisals. The UN and other Western NGOs said they would not deploy in Marjah because the US Army was running the reconstruction and the aid agencies' neutrality would be jeopardised.

As a result of this debate, the military became its development organisation – a mistake that would get worse over time because it could provide neither sustainability nor longevity for projects. In a special program run by the Pentagon, US commanders in the field were given cash to carry out quick-impact projects in their areas of command so that they could influence local people.

For the Commanders Emergency Response Program, a budget of $40 million was initially set aside. By 2008, this had grown to $750 million and by 2010, it was $1billion, which is more than the entire revenue of the Karzai government. Nobody was consulted on how these vast free-flowing funds were to be spent. The money was spent by military personnel without professional experience or knowledge, and without consultations with the relevant Afghans or civilian aid experts.

In the flat, irrigated lands on both sides of the Helmand River, the Taliban's best weapons were IEDs. Despite a $17 billion US military program to counter them, IEDs use and lethality had dramatically grown. The ammonium nitrate fertiliser used in the bombs, the trigger mechanisms, and other parts came almost wholly from Pakistan, but despite frequent US appeals, the Pakistanis did not attempt to shut down the manufacturers-even though the Pakistani Taliban's bombs used the same materials and parts.

The Taliban also knew that Marines would target Kandahar next, and attempted to destabilize the city with daily bomb blasts.

Therefore, the Taliban devised a strategy hoping to alienate people the least yet still squeeze the insurgents out of the city. Around 28,000 NATO forces, 10,000 Afghan troops, and 5,000 police were deployed in and around Kandahar – by far the largest military mission so far. Afghan troops were stationed inside the city of 2 million people, while the US Marines set up check posts on the outskirts. As both civilian and military causalities rose and air strikes inadvertently killed more civilians than militants, President Karzai became increasingly angry at the Coalition forces.

It had also become unsafe to travel the critical Kabul-Kandahar highway, where corrupt police, criminal gangs, and Taliban ran checkpoints.

The Taliban held enclaves in provinces around Kabul, such as Logar, Wardak, and Kapisa, from which they could terrorise the largely pro-government population. NATO offered no corresponding security. Moreover, the still weak Afghan army could have been better used to secure these areas, because many of its recruits come from these same provinces.

By 2011, the crises in Kabul and the seven provinces that surround the city had become far worse. Large areas (including towns) were under Taliban control, and development work had come to a standstill.

Taliban who was sheltering in these provinces could easily launch sporadic attacks in Kabul, such as the suicide attack on Intercontinental Hotel in June 2011 (which killed twenty-one people) and the brazen attack on the US embassy on September 13 (which killed twenty-seven people).

Stability in the Afghan heartland had steadily eroded, even though it was pivotal to a successful withdrawal of Western troops.

The Taliban were not the only problem. An added destabilising element according to an influential report was the nexus between criminal enterprises, insurgent networks, and corrupt political elites, which had been undermining Kabul's security and that of the central-eastern corridor. Outside these networks became in effect a Taliban shadow government and a hallmark of its progress. Shadow governors operated in more than half (thirty-five) of the sixty-two districts in the seven provinces. They ran a parallel government, collected taxes, administered justice, settled disputes, and appointed local leaders, sometimes just a few miles from the outskirts of Kabul. The United States had no plan or troops to combat this steady take over by the Taliban,

Afghans argued that NATO's surge in the south had increased the levels of violence, destabilized the entire country, and given the Taliban a propaganda boost.

In the meantime, the Coalition was finally bringing Afghan State Forces up to speed, in terms of numbers, equipment, training and mentoring. The Afghan Army reached its first target of 134,000 men in late 2010 and would expand further. The police would eventually number 126,000, although they were less well-trained. By October 2012, the Afghan State forces would total 352,000. In 2010, the United States spent $11 billion on the Afghan Security Forces – the largest single ticket item in the US defence budget.

In 2011, the Americans spent $11.6 billion on the Afghan Security Forces, equipping the army with armour and vehicles, and in 2012 the United States would spend $12.8 billion, after which there would be a rapid drawdown of expenditures. According to projections, by the end of 2012, the Americans would have spent a total of $39 billion building up the Afghan State Forces.

The Afghan claimed that it would cost $6 billion a year to maintain all these forces after 2014 – a bill that the Americans would have to pay, as the entire Afghan state income in 2014 would not be more than $3 billion.

But worrying downsides naturally affected the ability of the Afghan State Forces to take on the Taliban. In early 2011, the annual attrition rate from the Afghan Army was still a staggering 24 per cent: that is, one in seven newly enlisted soldiers was deserting. Eighty-six per cent of the soldiers were illiterate, and drug taking was an endemic problem. The police were even worse. Around 5,000 deserted or 3 per cent of the army, and there were no punishments for desertion. The real problem was the lack of leadership and the absence of a properly trained officer corp.

In the 1980s, when the Communist Afghan Army fought the mujahideen, there were similar large-scale desertions by rank-and-file soldiers, but the army held together because it had a core of dedicated Communist Pashtun Officers who were well-trained by the Soviets. The Pashtun officer class had now disappeared.

Although 80 per cent of the army units were now partnered with NATO units, no single Afghan Army unit was ready to take full responsibility.

The United States started a mass literary campaign within the army so that soldiers could at least read basic instructions. The Americans were doing all this during an insurgency and a US surge. By contrast, when the US started in Iraq in 2007, the Iraq security forces already outnumbered one million men. In a highly controversial part of the US buildup of security forces, the officials insisted on creating *arbaki,* or local self-defence forces in the villages. The Kabul government opposed the plan because it would allow warlords and militias to return to the countryside. The officials ran their arguments on the Sons of Iraq program, where 10,000 militiamen had been raised. They finally won support for their plan from Karzai and Obama. The officials planned to raise 30,000 men, but the Pashtun rural population was deeply suspicious of the militias. The program essentially put too many ill-disciplined armed men in the field.

Moreover, when the Afghan administrative presence in the province was so small, there were limits to what the ASF could achieve. The training of an Afghan civil service over the past ten years was an even worse tale of Western neglect, lack of Afghan interest, and short age of funds and expertise. There is now a civil service academy turning bureaucrats, but it will be years before they make a difference. The justice system was equally depleted, so the Taliban were easily able to exercise their form of justice in the countryside. One hundred and seventeen districts were without a single judge. Years on, no government ministry was fully competent to run its budget or organise its personnel or spending program. All the ministers lacked the capacity, trained officials, and ability to handle money.

The dependence on foreigners was enormous. In 2011, three hundred foreign advisers were still working at the interior ministry, costing the US government $36 million a year.

*****

In 2011, relations between the United States and Pakistan

were utterly breaking down, even as the levels of violence escalated in Pakistan and Afghanistan. The two countries differing interests collide daily. While the United States asked for the elimination of all extremist groups on Pakistani soil, the army insists on maintaining the Taliban and the Haqqani network until a suitable Afghan settlement had been reached that satisfies the Pakistan military.

According to Ayaz Amir, the Pakistani military has failed to notice that its options are becoming fewer as the country subsides into chaos; and fails to grasp that US unilateralism will necessarily increase, in the shape of military actions and possibly sanctions to degrade the Taliban and the Haqqani network. Instead, Pakistan's generals bury their heads in the sand and pretend no such threat will materialise and that the brinkmanship they pursue with the Americans can continue indefinitely. Their position is that if they cannot get what they want out of an Afghan settlement, nobody will get Afghan peace. Blinded by ideology, they resist any forward-looking strategic thinking. Pakistan's military does not want to deliver peace except on its terms; its civilians have no hope for reform without it. The ISI should be under no illusion it will be able to influence, much less control, anything in post-American Afghanistan.

Even as they wished the Americans would leave Afghanistan, the army also wanted them to stay because of a consistently profitable venture Washington had become for the military. The army receives more than $2 billion every year in various kinds of military aid from the United States, and losing that could prove to be destabilising for the army itself. But it was clear in 2009, that the economic crises in the West would determine how long the Western forces would stay on.

The United States, too, lacks a strategic vision for Afghanistan and the region that it could share or discuss with Pakistan. However, nobody knows what Americans want in the longer term.

The Americans appear to have made little effort to calculate the repercussions of unilateral military action: that Pakistan could become even more belligerent and that a final rupture could take place. At times, both sides seem to have an underlying death wish – both have had enough of the relationship, both are defiant, yet each the other; neither wants to revive the relationship under false pretences, yet neither can muster enough vision or assume responsibility to discuss a new paradigm. At times, each side convinces itself that it can do without the other, which of course is dreaming.

For Pakistan and the elite, much more is at stake than worsening relations with the United States. A huge economic crisis – economic, social, and political- that has been building since Musharraf's time is erupting. A particularly troubling sign is the escalating intolerance of non-Muslim minorities – an index of the rapid deterioration in the very idea of Pakistan.

When Jinnah founded the country, the white stripe down the side of Pakistan's green flag represented the minorities or non-Muslims, whom the majority Muslim population would protect or treat as equal citizens. Yet Christians who can afford to do so are now leaving the country in droves because of their persecution. The Ismailis, a Shia sect led by Agha Khan, have seen their professional and business class targeted by extremists.

In 2010 and 2011, Sunni extremists killed more than five hundred Shias, many of them Hazaras from Afghanistan who live peacefully in Baluchistan province.

The extremists want to redefine the state of Pakistan as an Islamic jihadist venture, and for that, they must create an atmosphere of total intolerance. Ayaz Amir once wrote: 'In our journey towards nationhood, we eschewed the rational and chose to play with the semantics of religion. What Pakistan has become today, a fortress not so much of Islam as of bigotry and intolerance is a fruit of these sustained endeavours.'

The most immediate issue is the controversial and outdated law on blasphemy, which many in the ruling Pakistan People's Party want to reform. The law is a catch – 22 because it allows anyone to charge anyone else with blasphemy, which leads to automatic arrest by the police. Yet, the charge or proof of it can never be named because it is blasphemous. At any given time, more than a thousand people are in jail, on charges of blasphemy, some Christian but many Muslims.

Moreover, Baluchistan, Pakistan's poorest and most neglected province is home to an insurgency as radical but secular Baluch leaders demand separation from Pakistan. The Baluch tribes have rebelled against the Pakistan army five times since 1947, but each time the insurgency has been put down brutally; that has only further alienated the Baluch while their political and economic grievances remain unaddressed. In August 2006, the army killed Nawab Abkar Khan Bugti, a powerful tribal chief and politician, and thirty of its men, which triggered a wider insurgency. When Zardari came to power in 2008, he promised reconciliation talks with the Baluch militants, but there have been no follow-up and no talks, and the insurgency had become more violent.

The fighting has been low-key but brutal. While Baluch militants have targeted the security forces with ambushes, assassination, and land mines, they have also killed non-Baluch settlers, including shopkeepers, teachers, and bureaucrats. Non-Baluchs have fled the province. Amnesty International and Human Rights Watch have described a 'kill and dump' policy, by which the security forces pick up, detain, torture, and kill the Baluch nationalists, activists, and ordinary civilians and students. Their bullet-ridden bodies are dumped on the roadside at a rate of about twenty a month.

In October 2010, Amnesty International issued a damning report demanding that the government investigate the torture and killings of more than forty Baluch leaders and political activists over the past four months. Human Rights Watch says that hundreds of Baluch have disappeared since 2005.

Increasingly, the Pakistani military has viewed the Baluch insurgency through the myopic lens of the Indian presence in Afghanistan, rather than treating it as a political issue. Pakistan claims that the RAW – India's intelligence agency is arming and funding the Baluch insurgents from Indian consulates in Afghanistan. As early as 2007, former president Musharraf told the Americans that a hostile India was arming the Baluch from Kabul. India denies the charge. In all past Baluch insurgencies, India has had a hand in providing some level of support – usually money for the insurgents in a tit-for-tat return for Pakistan's support for Kashmiri militants. There is every reason to suspect that India is also involved in this insurgency, possibly providing money to Baluch insurgent leaders who are living in Europe and the Gulf emirates. However, these facts still do not deter the Baluch from their central position that they have been poorly treated, their grievances have not been addressed, and there is no political process by which they can be heard in the corridors of power in Islamabad.

The disappearances of hundreds of people by the intelligence agencies in Baluchistan, even by military units such as the Frontier Corps, reflect the utter failure of the judiciary. The judiciary is a broken instrument incapable of handing down judgments to real criminals. A US State Department report says that in Pakistan, three in four defendants on terrorism charges are acquitted, either because the prosecutors lack proof or because the judges are intimidated. The failure of the courts has frustrated the military, which has increasingly taken the law into its own hands, summarily jailing or executing not just anti-state extremists but any political opponents of the army or the ruling party.

The city of Karachi is another fast-burning fuse that could detonate the entire country. Karachi is an extraordinary metropolis, one of the great economic engines of South Asia- holding the country's major port, its stock market, and more than half of its industry. Its 18 million people generate 70 per cent of the country's revenue and 30 per cent of the GDP, but every year its ethnic melting pot – the majority Mohajir community, who are settlers from India; Pashtun and Baluch tribesmen; Punjabi businessmen; and smaller groups from all over South Asia – are mired in ethnic violence. Mafias, criminal gangs, car thieves, and Taliban and sectarian extremists all carry out their turf wars and protection of rackets. The kinds of violence Karachi witnessed are seen nowhere else in Pakistan – targeted mass killings and torture using electric drills. Victims' heads, genitals, and limbs have been severed, stuffed into sacks, and dropped on the road. Every year since the 2009 election, an average of 1,200 people has been killed. An orgy of violence erupted in the summer of 2011 when around 300 people were killed.

The ethnic ghettos have become so entrenched and fortified that even Karachi ambulance services must send out drivers of the same ethnicity as the victim or they could get killed. The Taliban, with their thousands of madrassa students, could quite easily take over parts of Karachi when they feel the time is right. The MQM had been constantly talking about separating urban Karachi and Hyderabad from Sind province and creating a Singapore-like state – a move that would, however, lead to a civil war with the rural Sindhis.

Karachi port is also the main gateway for supplies for US and NATO troops in Afghanistan.

After 2001, almost 80 per cent of all military goods destined for the Afghan war were sent to Karachi and then trucked up to the border crossings in northwestern Pakistan. Now with new routes through Central Asia, the Karachi port caters to only 50 per cent of the goods, and that proportion was diminished further by the end of 2011. The economic impact would be significant with the loss of customs revenues, transport contracts, and jobs. Karachi is a microcosm of what is wrong with the country – the growing weakness of the state, the breakdown of the social contract, ethnic conflict, and the growing war between modernity, business liberalism, and extremism. These divisions will only get worse if the country dissolves into further lawlessness.

But the most pressing issue that will determine Pakistan's future and especially its relationship with the United States, is the economy. The country is extremely dependent on American goodwill for its economic survival – even beyond the nearly \$3 billion in annual military and economic aid that it has received since 2001. It also needs the United States to maintain its loans from primary lenders such as IMF, the World Bank, the Asian Development Bank, the European Union, and Japan.

A confrontation with the United States could mean that Pakistan loses \$4.8 billion annually in foreign assistance; moreover, according to top economist Akmal Hussain, the capital would flee abroad.

Over one-third of the population has been living below the poverty line, and the majority is deprived of basic services.

The economy has been tanking, with low GDP growth, high inflation, a huge fiscal deficit, and up to sixteen hours daily of no electricity – all of which have helped to reduce production and increase joblessness.

Since the 1980s, Pakistan's revenues had never been sufficient even to meet current expenditures; the entire development budget has been financed through foreign loans. Debt servicing and defence now take up some 60 per cent of the budget. Borrowing from abroad or from the State Bank has become a norm. Since 1988, Pakistan had sought bailouts from the IMF eleven times, yet it has failed to complete any IMF programs, except for one in 2001. 'Instead of seriously tackling fundamental problems of source scarcity', says Maleeha Lodhi, 'the government is embarked on doing more of the same – borrowing its way out of a dire situation…This approach always seems to be reaching a dire end.'

Islamic extremists had wisely made the dire condition of the economy and inflation a very effective rallying cry, targeting the government for its widespread corruption and waste, raising the issue of rich versus poor, and emphasising the Islamic way of sharing wealth versus dependence on loans from the West.

These multiple crises were arising as Pakistan's relations with the United States decayed.

The CIA – ISI relationship was now also speeding downwards. The Pakistani military had many times told CIA officers to leave the country, as well as US special forces trainers with the Frontier Corps. The military demanded a halt to all drone strikes and severely restricted issuing of visas to US officials.

The ISI aimed to strip the CIA of its clandestine operations in the country, while it whipped up further their anti-Americanism in the media by leaking fears that the United States wanted to undermine Pakistan's nuclear weapons capability.

Despite Pakistan's objections, the United States pressed ahead with the drone strikes. The pall of secrecy that the CIA cast over the drone strikes fuelled the worst suspicions among Pakistanis and Afghans and tended to mitigate whatever US soldiers were doing on the ground to win hearts and minds. Controversy erupted over the number of civilian causalities caused by these strikes, something that can never be settled if the CIA does not explain its criteria for choosing targets. Who exactly the CIA is aiming to kill is unknown, and what is legal US or international rights it must do so are also unknown.

The Pakistani military's growing belligerence toward the United States had been matched by a collapse of US confidence in Pakistan. In an April 2011 report to Congress, the White House said that Pakistan had made no effort to support Obama's troop surge and that the army had failed to defeat the Pakistani Taliban. The army tried three times to eliminate militants from the Mohamand tribal agency in FATA, which was, said the report, 'a clear indicator of the inability of the Pakistani military and government to render cleared areas resistant to insurgency return.'

The plight of FATA, after years of war, was described by Abubakar Siddique, the region's most renowned journalist: 'More than one million FATA residents remain displaced by the conflict. Tens of thousands of Pakistani soldiers continue to battle scores of militants.

Thousands have died in a seven-year insurgency in the region, with traditional tribal leaders either assassinated or chased from their home areas. FATA's status as Pakistan's backwater persists, with health, education, and other human development indicators among the lowest in Asia. And its strategic location and role as an extremist sanctuary promise to keep it embroiled in the insurgency.'

The promise of political reform in FATA had been held out to its people since 2001, but nothing had been achieved by successive governments. FATA desperately needed to become a part of the Pakistani state by a grant of provincial status or by joining KP province. Its British-based laws needed to be brought into line with Pakistani law and the services are given to the people of Pakistan, such as education and healthcare, needed to be made available to the FATA tribesmen.

***

UNKNOWINGS OF THE PAST

In 2009 Barack Obama stood before an adoring crowd in Prague and promised to make the world free from nuclear weapons. This was front-page news. Obama, in his tenure, approved an arsenal of nuclear weapons costing $350 billion, a record. This was not news.

Unleashed American generals reminiscent of those in Stanley Kubrick's *Dr. Strangelove,* now openly talk about a nuclear war with Putin's Russia. One of them was General Breedlove, who repeatedly said that Ruskies are massing and threatening. A barrage of similar threats and accusations has been aimed at China, increasingly. Perpetual war has become an idiom for those in American universities and media who describe themselves as 'liberal realists.'

Propaganda is the principal weapon at this stage, news is a smear and scare campaign of the kind, bringing back the days of the first cold war. The Russian president has been a pantomime villain, who can be abused with impunity.

Among the drumbeaters, there is the *joie d'spirit* of a class reunion. The liberal realists are the same people who, in promoting an invasion of Iraq, in 2003, declared the existence of Saddam's weapons of mass destruction to be hard facts.

As many as a million men, women, and children died therefore, and their ruined society converted to a breeding place for fanatics known as the Islamic State.

In the Caucasus and Eastern Europe, the biggest military buildup, since the Second World War is subjected to the most successful news blackout, along with Washington's effective takeover of the Russian borderland in Ukraine and the role of neo-Nazi brigades in terrorising the Russian-speaking population of eastern Ukraine.

'If you wonder', wrote Robert Parry, 'how the world could stumble into World War Three – much as it did into World War One a century ago – all you need to do is look at the madness that has enveloped virtually the entire US political/media structure over Ukraine where a false narrative of white hats versus black hats brewed up, and has proved impervious to facts or reason.

Parry, the journalist who revealed the Iran-Contra scandal is one of the few who has investigated the media's central role in this 'game of chicken', as the Russian Foreign Minister called it.

The rulers of the world want Ukraine not only as a military and missile base, but they also want its economy.

The US wants Ukraine for its abundant gas. Vice President Biden's son is on the board of Ukraine's biggest oil, gas, and fracking company.

The manufacture of GM seeds, companies such as Monsanto, want Ukraine's rich farming soil.

Above all, they want Ukraine's mighty neighbour, Russia They want to Balkanise or dismember Russia and exploit the greatest source of natural gas on earth.

As Arctic ice melts, they want to control the Arctic Ocean, its energy riches, and Russia's long Arctic land border.

Their man in Moscow used to be Boris Yeltsin, a drunk, who handed his country's economy to the West.

His successor, Putin, has reestablished Russia as a sovereign nation which is his crime.

In the nineteenth century, the Russian writer Alexandar Herzen described Western secular liberalism as 'the final religion, though its church is not the other world this.' Today, this divinity is far more violent and dangerous than anything the Muslim world throws up. In his celebrated essay 'On Liberty,' to which modern Western liberals pay homage, John Stuart Mill wrote: 'Despotism is a legitimate mode of government in dealing with barbarians, provided the end to be their improvement and the means justified by actually effecting the end.'

It is a nice and convenient myth that liberals are peacemakers and conservatives the warmongers, wrote the historian Hywel Williams in 2001, but the imperialism of the liberal way may be more dangerous because of its open-ended nature: its conviction that it represents a superior form of life.

Richard Falk, the respected authority on international law and the UN special rapporteur on Palestine, once described a 'self-righteous, one way, legal/moral screen with positive images of Western values and innocence portrayed as threatened, validating a campaign of unrestricted political violence. It is so widely accepted as to be virtually unchallengeable.

In the news, whole countries are ordained for their usefulness or expendability, or they are made to disappear.

The machinations of Saudi Arabia, a principal source of

extremism and Western-designed terror, is of minimal news interest, except when it wilfully drives down the price of oil.

Yemen has endured twelve years of American drone attacks and is now an American-backed Saudi invasion. This bloodletting has none of the thrall of Islamic State, a product of the destruction of Iraq, Libya, and Syria – just as Pol Pot and the Khmer Rouge were the product of the genocidal bombing of Cambodia.

Latin America has also suffered this western disappearing trick. In 2009, the University of the West of England published the results of a ten-year study of the BBC's coverage of Venezuela. Of 304 broadcast reports, only three mentioned any of the positive policies introduced by the government of Hugo Chavez. The greatest literary programme in human history received barely a passing reference.

In Europe and the United States, millions of readers and viewers know the text to nothing about the life-giving changes implemented in Latin America, many of them inspired by Chavez. Like the BBC, the reports of the *New York Times*, the *Washington Post*, the *Guardian*, and the rest of the respectable Western media were often notoriously in bad faith. Chavez was mocked even on his deathbed.

Why are millions of people in Britain persuaded that a collective punishment called 'austerity' is necessary? Following the economic crash in 2008, a rotten empire of capital was exposed. Banks were shamed as collective crooks with obligations to the public they had betrayed.

But, within months – apart from a few stones lobbed over excessive corporate bonuses – the media message had changed and public money diverted.

The mug shots of guilty bankers vanished from the newspapers and this new propaganda buzzword, austerity, became a burden for millions of ordinary people.

Today, many of the premises of civilised cultural life in Britain are being dismantled. The austerity cuts are said to be one hundred eighty-three billion American dollars, which is almost exactly the amount of tax avoided by the banks and by corporations like Amazon and Murdoch's News UK. Moreover, the banks are given an annual subsidy of a hundred billion pounds in free insurance and guarantees: a figure that would fund the entire National Health Service.

The economic crises are pure propaganda, a conjuring trick by the rulers of the world, led by corporate and media class warriors whose information dominance and control of the narrative – to quote the jargon of the realists – is their most powerful weapon.

Within a few years, driven by forces of consumerism and profit, the cult of me-ism had all but overwhelmed our sense of acting together, of social justice, and the welfare of all and internationalism. Class, gender, and race were separated. The personal was political, and the media was the message.

Today, the promotion of bourgeois privilege is often described as feminism. In 2008, the elevation of a man of colour to the presidency of the United States was celebrated as a blow against racism, even in the dawn of a post-racial era.

When a BBC presenter described Hillary Clinton as a

beacon of female achievement on 'Woman's Hour', she did not remind her listeners about her profanity that it was morally right to invade Afghanistan to liberate Afghan women.

She asked Clinton nothing about her part, as US secretary of state, in a terror campaign using drones to kill women, men and children. There was no mention of Clinton's idle threat while campaigning to be the first US female president, to eliminate Iran and nothing about her support for mass surveillance and pursuit of whistle-blowers.

Her husband, then President Clinton had invaded Haiti, and bombed the Balkans, Africa and Iraq, and it was of no interest. UNICEF had reported the deaths of half a million Iraqi infants, under the age of five because of an embargo, led by the US and Britain.

The children were media unpeople, just as Hillary Clinton's victims in the invasions she had promoted – Afghanistan, Iraq, Yemen, Somalia – were all unpeople.

In the politics, such as in journalism and arts, dissent once tolerated in the mainstream has regressed to a dissidence: a metaphoric underground. The recent seventieth anniversary of the liberation of Auschwitz was a reminder of the great crime of fascism, where Nazi iconography is embedded in our consciousness.

Fascism is preserved as history, as flickering footage of goose-tempering black shirts, their criminality terrible and clear.

Yet, in the same liberal societies, whose war-making elites urge us never to forget, the accelerating danger of a modern kind of fascism, is suppressed, for it is their fascism.

It was the Red Army that had destroyed most of the Nazi war machine, at the cost of as many as thirteen million soldiers. By contrast, US losses, in the Pacific, were four hundred thousand. But Hollywood has reversed it with their propaganda.

What we need is a Fifth Estate: a journalism that monitors, deconstructs, and counters propaganda, and teaches the young to be agents of people, not power. What is needed is what the Russians called as *perestroika*. Vandana Shiva calls this an insurrection of subjugated knowledge.

The responsibility for the rest of us is clear. It is to identify and expose lies of those who control the narrative, warmongers especially, and never to collude with them.

It is reawakening the great popular movements that brought a fragile civilisation to modern imperial states.

***

The attacks of September 11, 2001, did not change everything, but accelerated the continuity of events, providing an extraordinary pretext for destroying social democracy.

The undermining of the Bill of Rights in the United States and the further dismantling of trial by jury in Britain and a plethora of related civil liberties are part of the reduction in democracy to electoral ritual: that is, competition between indistinguishable parties for the management of a single ideology state.

Central to the growth of this business state is the media conglomerates, which have unprecedented power, owning press and television, book publishing, film production, and databases, as *Time* magazine called it: politics by media, war by media, justice by media, even grief by media (Princess Diana).

The global economy is their most important media enterprise. The global economy is a modern Orwellian term.

On the surface, it is instant financial trading, mobile phones, McDonald's, Starbucks, and holidays booked on the Internet.

Beneath this gloss, it is the globalisation of poverty, a world where most human beings never make a phone call, and live on less than two dollars a day, where six thousand children die every day from diarrhoea because most of them do not have access to clean water.

In this world, unseen by most of us in the global north, a sophisticated system of plunder has forced more than ninety countries into structural adjustment programmes since the eighties, widening the gap between rich and poor as never before.

This is known as nation-building, and good governance by the 'quad' dominating the World Trade Organisation (the United States, Europe, Canada, and Japan), and the Washington triumvirate (the World Bank, the IMF, and the US Treasury) that controls even minute aspects of government policy in developing countries.

Their power derives largely from a non-repayable debt that forces the poorest countries to pay hundred million American dollars to Western creditors every day. The result is a world where an elite of fewer than a billion people controls eighty per cent of humanity's wealth.

Promoting this is the transnational media corporations, American and European that own or manage the world's principal sources of news and information.

They have transformed much of the information society into a media age where extraordinary technology allows the incessant repetition of politically safe information that is acceptable to the nation-builders.

In the West, we are trained to view other societies in terms of their usefulness or threat to us and to regard cultural differences as more important than the political and economic forces by which we judge ourselves. Those with unprecedented resources to understand this including many who teach and research in great universities suppress their knowledge publicly; perhaps never has there been such silence.

When a million people died violently in bringing the new global economy to Indonesia, the greatest massacre of the second half of the twentieth century was not so much news as a cause for celebration.

Suharto's ascendency was the West's best news in years. James Reston, the doyen of American columnists, told readers of the *New York Times* that the bloody events in Indonesia were a gleam of light in Asia.

In our universities, Indonesian scholars approved Suharto's big lie about a communist coup being the cause of the killings, while Western corporations anointed the regime's stability.

The silence lasted for more than a quarter of a century until it was broken by the cries of Suharto's victims in East Timor: a second genocide conducted with Western military backing.

In our age, the widely held belief among anti-globalisation campaigners that the state has withered away, is misguided, along with the view that transnational corporate power has replaced the state and, by extension, imperialism.

The capacity of the American military machine to smash impoverished countries is undisputed, conditional on the absence of American ground troops and their subjugation by local or allied forces.

The exception was Vietnam. Regardless of their B-52 bombers, napalm, chemical defoliants and weight of numbers, American troops could not match the knowledge and tenacity of a people prepared to see off an invader. This was their imperial lesson.

Thus, in Afghanistan, only a handful of Americans have been killed. *Mujahideen* commanders reported B-52s destroying villages too small to be marked on any map, with perhaps more than three hundred people killed in one night.

In a family of forty, only a small boy and his grandmother survived, reported Richard Lloyd Perry of *The Independent*.

Out of sight of the television cameras, at least three thousand seven hundred sixty-seven civilians were killed by US bombs between October 7 and December 10, an average of sixty-two innocent deaths a day, according to one study, and this is in a country where last annual budget - $83 million – was one-tenth the cost of a B-52 bomber.

Moreover, the change in Afghanistan is superficial. Women still dare not go unveiled, and warring feudalism reigns.

According to the then Minister of Justice, who was American installed in Afghanistan, the Taliban used to hang a victim's body in the public for four days, but her government believed that it was all right to hang a body for execution for a shorter time like fifteen minutes.

The truth about September 11 is that the killing of thousands of innocent people cannot be justified in America or anywhere else.

But for people such as David McKnight, an Australian journalist and academic, the killing of thousands of innocents in Afghanistan, in response, was the global equivalent of police raiding the hide out of the criminal, involving a violent confrontation that is sometimes unavoidable in apprehending criminals.

He did not mention that Afghan peasants have the same right to life as New Yorkers. The murderous demolition of their villages, with not a Taliban or al-Qaeda fighter in sight, is unavoidable.

In other words, certain human lives have greater worth than others, and the killing of one set of civilians is a crime. People such as Bin Laden and George W Bush have been sustained with an ancient lie.

They are also joined by history. The CIA's Operation Cyclone trained and armed at least thirty-five thousand zealots who then became Taliban and al-Qaeda.

As John Cooley writes in his definitive *Unholy Wars: Afghanistan, America, and International Terrorism,* then British Prime Minister Margaret Thatcher's

Government supported the American-funded *jihad* with full enthusiasm, much of it that was coordinated by an M16 officer in Islamabad. Osama Bin Laden was given full reign, but the cost to the American taxpayer was four billion American dollars.

The CIA swore, hand on heart that Osama Bin Laden had not worked for them. The truth is that the Bush family was up to its collective ears with Bin Laden's, and Cheney-Bush oil and gas junta, as Vidal once called them, had an agenda that begged many questions of the months preceding September 11 and the days and weeks that followed.

It was not a crime to murder more than half a dozen peasants with bombs dropped secretly and illegally in Cambodia, igniting an Asian holocaust. It was not a crime for Bill Clinton and George Bush, Tony Blair, and his Tory predecessors, to have caused death in Iraq of more people than have been killed by all weapons of mass destruction in history, according to an American study.

A report by the United Nations Secretary-General in October 2001 says that the obstruction of $4 billion of humanitarian supplies by the US and British governments was by far the main cause of the extreme suffering and deaths in Iraq.

The United Nations Children's Fund, UNICEF, says that the death rate for under-fives almost trebled since 1990, before the imposition of sanctions, and every month up to six thousand children have died mostly because of the blockade. This is twice the total number of deaths in the Twin Towers and another vivid reminder of the different values of different lives. The Twin Towers' victims are people. The Iraqi children are unpeople.

Richard Perle, a cold war planner in the Reagan administration has explained the stances in this total war. He believes that they are fighting a variety of enemies, and there are lots of them out there.

But there are people from the opposite side, whose actions shame the silent, and defy the myth of apathy.

They belong to what the great American reporter Martha Gellhorn called an old and unending worldwide company, the men and women of conscience and struggle. Some are famous like Tom Paine, Wilberforce and Mandela, but most are little known in the West. In India, there are three hundred thousand strong, all-female Self-Employed Women's Association (SEWA); in Brazil the Landless Peoples Movement, in Mexico, the Zapatistas.

Their victories, usually recognised in the West, are often epic. In Bolivia's third city, Cochabamba, ordinary people took back their water from a corporate conglomerate, after the World Bank had pressurised the Bolivian government into privatising the public water supply.

Having refused credit to the public water company, the bank demanded that a monopoly be given to Aguas del Tunari, part of International Water Limited, a British-based company half owned by the American engineering giant Bechtel.

Granted a forty-year concession, the company immediately raised the price of water. In a country, where the minimum wage is less than $100 a month, people faced increases in their water bills of $20 a month – more than water users pay each month in the wealthy suburbs of Washington, home to many World Bank economists. In Cochabamba, even collecting rainwater without a permit was now illegal.

The epic struggle of journalists in Turkey for a free press, of trade unionists in Colombia, and the new tiger unions in East Asia are of no concern to us.

In Indonesia, the IMF may have delivered an expedient *coup de grace,* to the genocidal regime of Suharto, but it was brave people, like Dita Sari and Daniel Indra Kusuma, who broke the silence and faced guns and armoured vehicles, supplied by the dictator's friends, notably the British government.

In South Africa, it was the young people, like those in Soweto in 1976, who faced the Hippos, the armoured vehicles from which the police killed and wounded indiscriminately.

Study Paul Weinberg's historic photograph of a lone woman standing defiant between two of these monsters, as they rolled into her township; her arms are raised, and her fists are clenched. The negotiators played a part, but it was those like her who defeated apartheid.

The list is endless. Contrary to myth, people are seldom compliant. In a survey of thirty countries, Gallup found that the majority opposed the bombing of Afghanistan and military violence as a means of bringing extremists to justice. Most understand that real terror is poverty, from which some twenty-four thousand people die every day.

In the United States, where a military plutocracy rules, another generation now marches in streets that some of the most tenacious peace and democracy movements once filled.

In Europe, the energy and organisation are well ahead of the 1960s, rather like the blossoming political awareness of all sorts of people, especially the young.

They no longer confuse the distractions of elective oligarchies with true politics. Under many banners, this new endless company drawing millions from across the world may well be the greatest.

***

From the air, it is the industrial design of the city that is striking. Jakarta is ringed by vast, guarded, relatively modern compounds, known as export processing zones, or EPZs.

These enclose hundreds of factories that make products for foreign companies: the clothes people buy in high street Britain, in shopping malls in north America and Australia: from the high street designer look of Gap to the Nike, Adidas and Reebok trainers that sell in London's Oxford Street for up to 100 GBP a pair.

In these factories are thousands of workers earning the equivalent of seventy-two pence a day, about a dollar.
This is the official minimum wage in Indonesia, which says the government, is about half the living wage, and here a mere subsistence, bordering on a working pauperism.

Nike workers get about four per cent of the retail price of the shoes they make, which is not enough to buy laces. Still, they count themselves lucky: they have jobs. The booming, dynamic economic success has left more than thirty-six million Indonesians without work.

More than a thousand mostly young women work battery style, under the glare of strip lightening, in temperatures that reach forty degrees Centigrade. Their faces are silent, their eyes downcast, and their limbs move robotically.

The women have no choice about the hours they must work, including a notorious long shift of thirty-six hours without going home.

They stay till the order is full. If they want to go to the toilet, they must be lucky. They are treated like animals because they must work all the time without saying a word.

Foreigners often come to these factories, but they are interested in quality control, and rate of production. They never ask about the working conditions. They do not even look at them.

Clinging to the factories, like the debris of a great storm, are the labour camps where these workers live: Hobbesian communities crammed in long dormitories made from breeze blocks, plywood packing cases, and corrugated iron. Like most of the humanity who are not touched by the delights of McDonald's and Starbucks, the Internet, and mobile phones, who cannot afford to eat enough protein and rarely make a phone call, these are globalisation's unpeopled.

They live with open, overflowing sewers and unsafe water; up to half of their wages go on drinkable water. Past their homes run stinking canals dug by former colonial masters, the Dutch, in the usual vainglorious attempt to recreate Europe in Asia. The result is an environmental disaster, today, a plague of them in the camps has brought a virulent form of dengue, known as break back fever.

For the malnourished young children in the camps, dengue can mean death. It is a disease of globalisation, as camps grew and people migrated from rural areas looking for work, the mosquitos followed them.

Many of the people had fled an impoverished system of cash cropping, devised by the World Bank, which has progressively wiped-out self-sustaining agriculture in much of Indonesia.

In one of the passageways, filled with clothes hanging in plastic, it was like a backroom of dry cleaners. The cleanliness and neatness of the people living in this warren are astonishing. They occupy cell-like rooms, mostly without windows or ventilation, in which eating and sleeping are tuned to the ruthless rhythm of shiftwork in the factories.

During the monsoon season, the canals rise and flood and more plastic materialise to protect possessions; a precious tape player, posters of the Spice Girls, and Che Guevara. I almost tipped over a frying pan of sizzling tofu. Open paraffin fires and children are darting perilously close. I watched a family of five perched on a patch of green, gazing at the sunset, through a polluted yellow haze; tiny bats circled overhead, and in the distance were the skeleton silhouettes of deserted skyscrapers. It was an apocalyptic glimpse of a globalised world unknown to those of us who consume.

The code of conduct that the company says it distributes to the contractors includes this: dormitory facilities must meet all applicable laws and regulations, related to health and safety, including fire safety, sanitation, risk protection, and electrical, mechanical, and structural safety.

Because these dormitories are not on the factory site, companies and their contractors are not liable.

Consumers in the West might reflect on this non-liability, as they pay for fashionable clothes, made by people who cannot afford a decent place, to live on the wages they are paid.

Ten miles from the camps, along the toll road owned by Suharto's daughter (he had distributed the national power grid among his children; banks, hotels, and vast tracts of forests were tossed to generals and cronies), lies in downtown Jakarta. This is, or was, the approved face of the 'modern pupil.'

***

The Gotham City skyline of downtown Jakarta is mostly banks, many of them empty, and unfinished buildings.

Before 1997, there were more banks here, than in any city on earth; half of them went bankrupt when the dynamic economy collapsed beneath the weight of its barely visible corruption.

During Suharto's thirty-year dictatorship, a cataract of global capital poured into Indonesia.

The World Bank had handed over more than thirty billion American dollars, some of which went on worthwhile programmes, like literacy. More than six hundred thirty million American dollars went into a notorious 'transmigration programme' that allowed the regime to colonise the archipelago.

Migrants from all over Indonesia were sent to occupied East Timor, where they soon controlled the economy.

In 2001, the bloodletting in Kalimantan (Borneo) was directed against Madura islanders, who had been shipped in to develop the territory under a World Bank scheme.

In August 1997, a secret World Bank report, written in Jakarta, disclosed the greatest scandal in the history of development – that at least twenty to thirty per cent of the bank loans are diverted through informal payments to Government of Indonesia staff and politicians.

During his dictatorship, seldom a day would pass when General Suharto was not being congratulated by Western politicians for bringing stability to the world's fifth most populous nation.

British politicians were especially appreciative, beginning with Harold Wilson's Foreign Secretary, Michael Stewart, who in 1966 lauded the dictator's sensible economic policies, and believed that the regime was not aggressive.

Margaret Thatcher had called Suharto one of his best and most valuable friends. John Major's Foreign Secretary had championed the regime's Asian values.

In 1997, Robert Cook's first trip abroad as Foreign Secretary included Indonesia, where he shook hands warmly with Suharto: so bizarrely, to illustrate the Foreign Office report on human rights in the world. Only the Australians, with their complex fears of their Asian neighbours, perceived as about to fall on them, as if by force of gravity, were more obsequious.

Then Prime Minister Bob Hawke believed that Suharto's people loved him. His successor, Paul Keating, the Australian press claimed, looked upon Suharto as a father figure, and had lauded him for creating a tolerant society and bringing stability to the region.

In 1996, then Deputy Prime Minister, Tim Fischer, declared that when magazines look for the man of the world of the second half of the century, they perhaps should not look much further than Jakarta.

They all knew of course that Amnesty almost filled a room with evidence of Suharto's ghastly record. Robin Cook was aware of an exhaustive investigation by the foreign affairs committee of the Australian Parliament that concluded that Suharto's troops had caused the death of at least two hundred thousand East Timorese, a third of the population.

In New Labour's first year in office, Britain was the biggest weapons supplier to Indonesia, with Blair approving eleven arms deals with Indonesia under cover of the Official Secrets Act and Cook's declaration of an ethical dimension to foreign policy.

This had a certain logic. The arms trade is one of globalisation's successes, and Indonesia has played a vital role. When the global economy (unfettered capitalism) took hold in Britain in the early 1980s, Margaret Thatcher set about dismantling much of the manufacturing and industry while restoring the British arms industry to a supremacy second only to the United States. This was done with veiled subsidies of the kind that routinely underwrite and rig the free market.

Almost half of all the research and development funds went on defence, and the Export Credit Guarantee Department of the Department of Trade and Industry offered soft loans to third-world regimes shopping for high-tech ammunition to rattle.

That many had appalling human rights records and internal conflict and/or were on the verge of war with a neighbour (India, Pakistan, Iran, Iraq, Israel) was not a barrier.

Indonesia was a major recipient of these virtual giveaways. During one twelve-month period, almost one billion of ECGD money financed the sale of Hawk fighter-bombers to Indonesia.

The unknowing British taxpayer paid up; the arms industry reaped its profits, and Hawks were used to bombing villages in the mountains of East Timor.

Some years ago, International Monetary Fund offered post Suharto government a rescue package of multi-million-dollar loans.

The conditions included the elimination of import tariffs on staple foods. Trade in all qualities of rice was been opened to general importers and exporters, decreed the IMF's Letter of Intent. Fertilisers and pesticides also lost their seventy per cent subsidy.

Due to this process, many farmers were likely to go bankrupt and their children were forced to work in the cities. Moreover, it gives green light to the giant American food grains corporations to move into Indonesia. The double standard embodied in these conditions is breathtaking.

Agribusiness in the West, especially in the United States and Europe, has produced its famous surpluses and export power only because of high tariff walls and massive domestic subsidies. The result has been a monopoly on humanity's staples.

Many Indonesian farmers were imprisoned when General Suharto, an opportunist, seized power in Indonesia in 1965-66, the year of living dangerously, eventually deposing the nationalist president Achmed Sukarno, who had led Indonesia since the end of Dutch colonial rule.

Estimates of the people who had died in a pogrom directly primarily at Indonesia's communist party, the PKI, range from five hundred thousand to more than a million.

For example, on Buru Island, thousands were imprisoned, at first without housing, food, and water. Many men were imprisoned because they refused to vote for Suharto's front party, Golkar.

However, in the post-Suharto era, many Indonesians are now overcoming a fear that has consumed a generation; and throughout the countryside, families have begun to excavate the remains of their loved ones. They are furtive figures of the night, occasionally glimpsed on the rim of a paddy, or a riverbank.

The older witnesses of the regime's violent acts recall rivers jammed with bodies like logs; in village after village, young men were slaughtered for no reason, their murders marked by rows of severed penises.

In terms of numbers killed, according to Central Intelligence Agency, the massacres rank as one of the worst mass murders in the Central Intelligence Agency's history. The historian Gabriel Kolko wrote that the final solution to the communist problem in Indonesia ranks as a crime of the same type that Nazis perpetrated. According to the Asia specialist Peter Dale Scott, Western politicians, diplomats, journalists, and scholars, some with prominent CIA connections, are perhaps principally responsible for the myth that Suharto and the military had saved the nation's honour from an attempted coup by the Indonesian communist party, the PKI, whose carnage had created a popular revulsion.

Since Suharto's fall, a body of evidence has been amassed that exposes the fiction both moderate regime and the communist carnage of 1965-66.

Witnesses have spoken for the first time and documents have become known strongly suggesting that Suharto, who had military command of Jakarta, exploited an internecine struggle, to seize power. Certainly, if it was a communist coup, it had a unique feature: none of its officers accused of plotting it was a communist. There is little doubt now that the pogrom was fanned by Suharto and his conspirators, and that PKI members and anybody who got in the way were the victims.

Between 1959 and 1965, more than fifteen million people joined political parties or affiliated mass organisations that were encouraged to challenge British and American influence in the region. With three million members, the PKI was the largest communist party in the world outside the Soviet Union and China.

In 1990, the American investigative journalist Kathy Kadane revealed the extent of secret American collaboration in the massacres of 1965-66 which allowed Suharto to seize the presidency. Following a series of interviews with former US officials, she wrote: 'They systemically compiled comprehensive lists of communist operatives. As many as five thousand names were furnished to the Indonesian army, and Americans later checked off the names of those who had been killed or captured.'

Joseph Lazarsky, the deputy CIA station chief in Jakarta, said that the confirmation of killings came straight from

Suharto's headquarters. The station was getting a good account in Jakarta of who was being picked up.

The army had a shooting list of about four thousand to five thousand people. They did not have enough goon squads to zap them all, and some individuals were valuable for interrogation. The infrastructure of the PKI was zapped immediately. Having already armed and equipped much of the army, Washington secretly supplied Suharto's troops with a field communications network as the killings got underway. Flown in at night by US air force planes based in the Philippines, this was state-of-the-art equipment, whose high frequencies were known to the CIA and the National Security Agency advising President Johnson.

Not only did this allow Suharto's generals to coordinate the killings, it meant that the highest echelons of the US administration were listening in and Suharto could seal off large areas of the country.

Although there is an archive film of people being herded into trucks, and driven away. A single fuzzy photograph, it is believed is the only pictorial record of what was Asia's holocaust. Ralph McGehee, a senior CIA operation officer in the 1960s described the terror in Indonesia from 1965 to 1966 as a model operation for the American-run coup that got rid of Salvador Allende in Chile seven years later. He wrote that the CIA forged a document purporting to reveal a leftist plot to murder Chilean military leaders. He even believed that Indonesia was also a model for Operation Phoenix in Vietnam, where American-directed death squads assassinated up to fifty thousand people.

Since the fall of Suharto in 1998, Indonesia has had a fragile secular parliamentary democracy. Under the new constitution, the army, which gave Suharto its power, during and after the bloodbath of 1965-66, has lost a significant number of privileges, notably a guaranteed block of seats in the parliament. Among senior officers, there is a huge sense of grievance. East Timor was the army's Vietnam, and its loss was resented deeply. The arrival of an Australian United Nations peacekeeping force was seen as the final humiliation.

In the pogroms of 1965-66, Suharto's generals often used Islamist groups to attack communists and anybody who got in the way.

A pattern emerged, whenever the army wanted to exert political authority, it would use Islamists in acts of violence and sabotage, so that sectarianism could be blamed and justify the inevitable crackdown – by the army.

When an Indonesian Garuda airliner was hijacked in 1982, Islamists were found to be responsible, but behind them was almost certainly an army faction.

In rebellious West Papua, in the past, the army openly supported an army group, Lashkar Jihad, while playing its traditional role of terrorising the local population to protect the vast multinational Freeport copper and gold mine, the world's largest. In Aceh, where American Exxon Company has holdings in oil, drilling and liquefied natural gas, human rights violations by the army are well documented.

***

Doctors have suspected depleted uranium, which was used, by Americans and British in the Gulf War across the southern battlefields of Iraq.

Under the economic embargo imposed by the United Nations Security Council in 1990, and upgraded the following year, Iraq is denied the equipment and expertise to decontaminate the battlefields, in contrast to how Kuwait was cleaned up after the Gulf War.

Some people have five thousand times more radiation in their bodies. The contamination was right through Kuwait and Iraq. With the munitions testing and preparations in Saudi Arabia, uranium contamination covers the entire region.

The effect depends on whether a person inhaled it, ingested it by eating and drinking, or they got it in an open wound. As the result, there are respiratory problems, kidney problems, and cancers as a direct result of this highly toxic material.

In the Gulf war, over three hundred tons were fired. An A-10 Warthog attack aircraft fired over nine hundred thousand rounds.

Each round was three hundred grams of solid uranium 238. When a tank fired its shells, each round carried over four thousand five hundred grams of solid uranium. These rounds are not coated, they are not tipped, and they are solid uranium. Moreover, there has been evidence that they have been mixed with plutonium. What happened in the Gulf War was a form of nuclear warfare.

The other issue is a denial of healthcare to American, British, and other allied soldiers, and tens of thousands of Iraqis were contaminated.

The Iraqis did not use depleted uranium; it was not their weapon. They simply do not know how to get rid of it from their environment.

The United Nations Sanctions Committee in New York, dominated by the Americans and the British, has vetoed or delayed a range of vital medical equipment, chemotherapy drugs, and even painkillers. The saddest thing is that it is the children who have been most affected because there is no chemotherapy and no pain control. It seemed crazy that they could not have morphine, because, for everybody with cancer pain, it is the best drug.

The UN Sanctions Committee had banned nitrous oxide as a weapon's dual use, yet this was used in caesarean sections to stop bleeding, and perhaps save a mother's life.

The amounts used would be so small that even if you collected all the drugs supply for the whole nation, and pooled it, it is difficult to see how anyone could make chemical warfare out of it.

The very provisions of the Charter of the United Nations and the Declaration of Human Rights have been set aside. There has been a war waged by the United Nations, on the children and people of Iraq, and with incredible results.

Saddam Hussein had not paid the price for economic sanctions. On the contrary, they had strengthened him.

It has been the little people who had lost their children, or their parents for things like untreated water.

For a while, it seems Security Council was out of control, for its actions, as it undermined its own Charter, the Declaration of Human Rights, and the Geneva Convention. History will teach a lesson to those who have been responsible.

After seeing the abject conditions, Hans Von Sponeck, who was Human Rights Coordinator in Baghdad and was an employee for the UN for thirty years, resigned.

 It was because she believed what was done to Iraqi people had never seen done before. After the resignation, two days later, Jutta Burghart, head of the World Food Programme, in Iraq, resigned as well, as she could not tolerate what was done to the Iraqi people.

***

When sanctions were imposed, following Iraq's invasion of Kuwait in August 1990, all imports, including food were effectively banned for eight months, even though Security Council Resolution 661 of August 6, 1990 explicitly exempted food and medicines.

For a year, the UN refused to allow Iraq the means for raising funds beyond its exhausted cash reserves. As Iraq imported almost everything, the effect was immediate and devastating, compounded by the results of a bombing campaign, designed to cripple civilian infrastructure.

According to *Washington Post*, US military planners hoped that the bombing would amplify the economic and psychological impact of international sanctions on Iraqi society. Because of these goals, damage to civilian infrastructure, and interests, invariably described by briefers during the war as collateral, and unintended was sometimes neither.

The worst civilian suffering had resulted not from bombs that went astray, but from precision-guided weapons that hit exactly where they were aimed – at electrical plants, oil refineries, and transportation networks.

Among the justifications given by a senior US air force officer was that Iraqi civilians were not blameless.

Reporting on the aftermath of the bombing, UN Under-Secretary-General Martti Ahtisaari described the near-apocalyptic state of the country's basic services. He once wrote that Iraq had for some time been relegated to a pre-industrial age, but with all the disabilities of post-industrial dependency on intensive use of energy and technology.

A Harvard University study team once concluded that Iraq was heading for a public health catastrophe with tens of thousands of deaths by the end of 1991 alone, most of them young children. The team of independent American professionals and academics estimated that during the first eight months of sanctions, when all the shipments were blockaded, forty-seven thousand children under the age of five had died.

The policymakers who had backed the sanctions cannot say that they did not know what was going to happen. Whatever the political decision, it was a conscious and callous choice to deny an entire society the means necessary to survive.

In 1991, the Security Council, in its Resolution 687, stated that, if Iraq renounced weapons of mass destruction (nuclear, biological, and chemical weapons), and ballistic missiles with a range of 150 kilometres, and agreed to be monitored by a UN Special Commission on Iraq (UNSCOM), the embargo would be lifted. In 1998, UNSCOM reported that despite Iraqi obstruction in some areas, the disarmament phase of the Security Council's requirements was possibly near its end in the missile and chemical weapons areas.

On December 15, 1998, the International Atomic Energy Agency reported that it had eliminated Iraq's nuclear weapons programme efficiently and effectively.

By 1998, the chemical weapons infrastructure had been completely dismantled or destroyed by UNSCOM, or by Iraq in compliance with the mandate. The biological weapons programme was gone, and all the major facilities were eliminated. The nuclear weapons programme was eliminated. The long-range ballistic missile programme was eliminated.

While food and medicines are technically exempt, the Sanctions Committee had frequently vetoed and delayed requests for baby food, agricultural equipment, heart and cancer drugs, oxygen tents, and X-ray machines. Sixteen heart and lung machines were put on hold because they contained computer chips.

A fleet of ambulances was held up because their equipment included vacuum flasks, which kept the medical supplies cold; vacuum flasks were designated dual use by the Sanctions Committee, meaning they could be used in weapons manufacture.

Cleaning materials such as chlorine, are dual use, as is the graphite used in pencils, as were the wheelbarrows, considering the frequency of their appearance on the lists of holds. As on October 2001, 1,010 contracts for humanitarian supplies, worth 3.85 billion American dollars, were on hold by the Sanctions Committee. They included items related to food, health, water and sanitation, agriculture, and education.

Most members of the Security Council wanted the sanctions eased or considerably lifted. The French have called them 'cruel, ineffective and dangerous'.

However, American dominance of the Council is such that the US and British representatives on the Sanctions Committee alone veto and delay contracts. The British had claimed to hold up only one per cent of the humanitarian contracts. This is a sophistry by never objecting to American obstruction, they give it tacit support. Moreover, a veto or a hold can only be rescinded by the Council member who orders it.

So blatant is the obstruction that Kofi Annan, the UN Secretary-General virtually appointed by the Americans, complained that the delays and vetoes were seriously impairing the effective implementation of the Oil for Food Programme.

He urged the approval of water, sanitation, and electricity contracts without delay because of their paramount importance to the welfare of the Iraqi people.

The Executive Director of the UN Office of the Iraq Programme, Benon Sevan, had attacked the Council for holding up spares for Iraq's crumbling oil industry, warning that the less oil Iraq can pump, the less money will be available to buy food and medicine.

In Britain, the Customs and Excise had stopped parcels going to Iraqi relatives, containing children's clothes and toys. The chairman of the British Library, John Ashworth, wrote to Harry Cohen MP that after consultation with the foreign office, it was decided that books could no longer be sent to Iraqi students.

The British Library had already distinguished itself by informing a translator in Baghdad that it was not permitted to send him a copy of James Joyce's *Ulysses*.

From the petty and craven to the farcical: an attempt to send documents to Iraq advising Iraqis on human rights and press freedom was blocked by the Department of Trade and Industry in London.

The package, which also contained advice on family planning and Aids, was posted to Mosul University but was intercepted and returned to Article 19, the anti-censorship group.

As most Iraqis have no other source of income, food has become a medium of exchange; it gets sold for other necessities, further lowering the calorie intake. You must get clothes and shoes for your kids to go to school. You have then got malnourished mothers, who cannot breastfeed, and they pick up bad water. What is needed is an investment in water treatment and distribution, electric power production for food processing, storage and refrigeration, education, and agriculture.

Oil for Food Programme allows hundred American Dollars for each person to live on for a year. This figure also must help pay for the entire society's infrastructure and essential services, such as power and water. It is simply not possible to live on that amount.

Set that pittance against the lack of clean water in the past, the fact that electricity had failed for up to twenty-two hours a day, and most sick people have not afforded treatment, and the sheer trauma of trying to get from day to day, and you have a glimpse of the nightmare.

And make no mistake, this was deliberate. Using the word genocide had become unavoidable.

The cost of lives is staggering. A study by the United Nations Children Fund, UNICEF found that between 1991 to 1998, there were five hundred thousand deaths above the anticipated rate among Iraqi children under five years of age. This, on average is five thousand two hundred times preventable under-five deaths per month.

In 1999, a humanitarian panel set up by the Security Council reported that Iraq had slipped from relative affluence before 1991 into massive poverty. The panel criticised the Oil for Food Programme as inadequate to remedy a dire humanitarian situation that cannot be overstated. The panel's members took a remarkable step of attacking their sponsor, charging that Iraqi people would not be undergoing such deprivations in the absence of the prolonged measures imposed by the Security Council. Once again, children were found to be the main victims, with the infant mortality rate soaring from one of the lowest in the world in 1990 to the highest.

The death rate of children in Iraq is unique. There is almost no documented case of rising mortality for children under five years of age in the modern world.

Extrapolating from these statistics, American researchers John Mueller and Karl Mueller conclude that economic sanctions have probably already taken the lives of more people in Iraq than have been killed by all weapons of mass destruction in history.

In 1999, seventy members of the US Congress signed an unusually blunt letter to President Clinton, appealing to him to leave the embargo and end what they call infanticide masquerading as policy. The Clinton administration had already given their reply. In 1996, in an infamous interview on the American current affairs programme *60 minutes,*

Madeleine Albright, then US Ambassador to the United Nations, had been asked why half a million children have died and were the price worth it. She replied that it was a very hard choice and the price was worth it.

***

After the oil was discovered in the late ninetieth century, the European powers lost no time in getting their hands on the greatest price. By 1918, they had seen off the Ottoman Turks and divided up the empire. Iraq and all the Arab lands became colonies, despite earlier promises of independence after the war. France kept Syria, Lebanon, and northern Iraq; Britain seized Baghdad and Basra in the south. The long-suffering Kurds were kept in a separate region under the British; and when they rose, Winston Churchill, the Colonial Secretary mused: 'I do not understand the squeamishness about the use of gas. I am strongly in favour of using poisoned gas against uncivilised tribes.'

Two years later, the Iraqi monarchy was overthrown by a nationalist, Abd al-Karim Kassem, who himself fell victim to an internecine struggle.

The new regime called itself an Arab socialist union, and a measure of plurality included a decentralised administration and recognition of the Kurdish language and national identity. When the Iraq Petroleum Company, the foreign consortium that exploited Iraq's oil, was threatened with nationalisation in 1963, the new imperial power, the United States engineered what the Central Intelligence Agency called its favourite coup.

James Critchfield, then head of the CIA in the Middle East regarded it as a great victory. The Secretary General of the Baath Party, Ali Saleh Saadi, concurred that they came to power on a CIA train, thereafter instigating a reign of terror that produced Saddam Hussein, who became the top man in 1979.

He was America's man. According to his biographer, Said Aburish, Saddam had a great deal to thank the CIA. American intelligence brought Baathists to power, helped Saddam personally, provided him with financial aid, during the war with Iran, and for protecting him against internal coups.

So enduring was America's ardour, or rather its gratitude for Iraq, for protecting its client Arab states from Iran's revolutionary guards that Saddam Hussein was given everything he wanted, almost up to the day he invaded Kuwait in August 1990.

When John Kelly, the US Assistant Secretary of State, visited Baghdad in 1989, she had regarded him as a force of moderation in the region, and that the United States wanted to broaden its relationship with Iraq.

Saddam Hussein, as a force of moderation, had just claimed victory in Iraq against Iran, which resulted in more than a million casualties from both sides, dead and wounded.

When human rights groups presented evidence that Saddam Hussein had used mustard gas and nerve gas against Iranian soldiers and Kurdish soldiers, the State Department refused to condemn him. As Saddam Hussein was preparing his forces for the attack on his southern neighbour, a US Department of Energy official discovered that advanced nuclear reactors were being shipped to Iraq. When he alerted his superiors, he was moved to another job. Americans knew about their bomb program, but Saddam was their ally.

In 1992, a Congressional inquiry found that President George Bush Senior and his top advisors had ordered a cover-up to conceal their secret support for Saddam Hussein and the illegal arms shipments being sent to him via third-world countries.

Missile technology was shipped to South Africa and Chile and then sold to Iraq, while Commerce Department records were altered and deleted. (This mirrored the emerging scandal across the Atlantic, which saw British weapons technology being illegally shipped to Iraq, with Jordan listed on Kuwait, the CIA was still feeding copious intelligence to Baghdad.

Congressman Henry Gonzalez, chairman of the House of Representatives banking committee believed that Bush and his advisors financed, equipped, and succoured Saddam, who they later went out to slay, and they were now burying the evidence.

A 1994 Senate report documented the transfer to Iraq of the ingredients of biological weapons: botulism developed at a company in Maryland, licensed by the Commerce Department and approved by the State Department. Anthrax was also supplied by the Porton Down laboratories in Britain, a government establishment. A Congressional investigator believed that it was all about money and greed, and they did not care. And there were running in competition with the Germans. That is how the arms trade works.

During the parallel Scott Inquiry in London into the arms to Iraq scandal, Tim Laxton, a City of London auditor, was brought in to examine the books of the British arms company, Astra, which the Thatcher Government covertly and illegally used as a channel for arms to Iraq.

Laxton was one of the very few observers to sit through the entire enquiry. He believed that if Sir Richard Scott's brief had been open and unlimited, and Thatcher's senior aides and civil servants had been compelled to give evidence under oath, as well as numerous other vital witnesses who were not called, the outcome would have been very different from the temporary embarrassment meted out to a few ministers.

Hundreds, he believed would have faced investigation, including top political figures, very senior civil servants from the Foreign Office, the Ministry of Defence, the Department of Trade, and the top echelon of government.

***

Before 1991, Baghdad's water was as safe as any water in the developed world. In times such as today, when it is left untreated, the water has become lethal. In fact, during the Christmas of 1999, the Department of Trade and Industry in London restricted the export of vaccines meant to protect Iraqi children against yellow fever and diphtheria

The scale of the bombings in no-fly zones is also astonishing. During the eighteen months to January 14, 2000, American air force and naval aircraft flew thirty-six thousand sorties over Iraq, including twenty-four thousand combat missions.

In 1999, American and British aircraft dropped more than eighteen hundred bombs and hit four hundred fifty targets. The cost to the British taxpayer was more than eight hundred million British pounds.

There was bombing almost every day. It was the largest Anglo-American aerial campaign since the Second World War, yet it was ignored by the British and American media.

In a rare acknowledgement, the *New York Times* reported that American warplanes had methodically and with virtually non-public discussion been attacking Iraq.

 Pilots had flown about two-thirds as many missions as NATO pilots flew over Yugoslavia in seventy-eight days of the around-the-clock war there.

The purpose of the no-fly zones, according to the British and American governments was to protect the Kurds in the north and the Shia in the south against Saddam Hussein's forces.

The aircraft was performing a vital humanitarian task, according to then Prime Minister Tony Blair, that would give minority peoples the hope of freedom and the right to determine their destinies.

Blair's specious words are given the lie by a secret history. When Saddam Hussein was driven from Kuwait, in 1991, his generals were surprised to be told by the victors that they could keep their helicopter gunships.

The British commander, General Sir Peter de la Billiere, defended this decision with an astonishing logic that the country's law and order would not be realised without helicopters.

Turkey, in the past, has been critical to the American

world order. Overseeing the oilfields of the Middle East and former Soviet Central Asia, it is a member of NATO and recipient of billions of dollars' worth of American arms. It is where American and British fighter bombs are based.

A long-running insurrection by Turkish Kurds, led by Kurdish Workers Party, is regarded by Washington as a threat to the stability of Turkey's crypto-fascist regime.

Following the Gulf War, the last thing that Americans wanted was tens of thousands of Iraqi Kurds arriving in Turkey as refugees and boosting the struggle of local Kurds against the regime in Ankara.

Their anxieties were reflected in Security Council Resolution 688, which warned of a massive flow of refugees towards and across the international frontiers, which threatens internal peace and security in the region.

What the refugees threatened was Turkey's capacity to continue to deny basic human rights to the Kurds within its borders. The northern fly zone offered a solution. Since 1992, the zones have provided cover for Turkey's repeated invasions of Iraq. In 1995 and 1997, as many as fifty thousand Turkish troops, backed by tanks, fighter bombers, and helicopter gunships, occupied swathes of the Kurds' haven, allegedly attacking PKK bases.

In December 2000, they were back, terrorising Kurdish villages and murdering civilians. The US and Britain, at that time, said nothing. The Security Council said nothing. Moreover, the British and Americans colluded in the invasions, suspending their flights to allow the Turks to get on with the killing.

Virtually none of this was reported in the Western media. In March 2001, RAF pilots patrolling the northern fly zone publicly protested for the first time about their role in the bombing of Iraq.

Far from performing the vital humanitarian task, described by Tony Blair, they complained that they were frequently ordered to return to their Turkish base to allow the Turkish air force to bomb the Kurds in Iraq, the very people they were meant to be protecting.

As per Dr Erric Herring, the Iraqi sanctions specialist at Bristol University, whenever the Turks wanted to mob the Kurds in Iraq, the RAF aircraft were recalled to base and ground crews were told to switch off their radar so that the Turk's target would not be visible. One British pilot reported seeing the devastation in Kurdish villages caused by the attacks when he resumed his patrol.

According to Dr Herring, they were very unhappy about what they had been ordered to do, and what they had seen, especially as there had been no official explanation.

In October 2000, the Washington Post reported that on more than one occasion, US pilots who fly in tandem with the British have received a radio message 'Turkish Special Mission' heading into Iraq. Following standard orders, the Americans turned their planes around and flew back to Turkey. When the Americans flew back into Iraqi air space, they would see burning villages, lots of smoke and fire.

During the Gulf War, President George Bush Senior called on the Iraqi military and the Iraqi people to take matters into their hands and force Saddam Hussein to step aside.

In March 1991, most Shia people in the south rallied to Bush's call and rose.

So successful were they, at first, that within two days, Saddam Hussein's rule had collapsed across Southern Iraq, and the popular uprising had spread to the country's second city, Basra.

A new start for the people of Iraq seemed nearby. Then the tyrant's old friends in Washington intervened just in time.

The opposition found themselves confronted with the United States helping Saddam Hussein against them. The Americans stopped rebels from reaching armed depots.

They denied them shelter, as per Said Aburish. They gave Saddam Hussein's Republican Guard safe passage through American lines to attack the rebels.

They did everything, except join the fight on the side. In their book, *Saddam Hussein: An American Obsession* Andrew and Patrick Cockburn describe the anguish of one of the rebel leaders, a brigadier, who watched American helicopters circulating overhead as Iraqi helicopter crews poured kerosene on fleeing refugees and set them alight with tracer fire.

In Nasiriyah, American troops prevented the rebels from taking guns and ammunition from the army barracks. The rebels eventually found a French colonel, who wanted to help; he tried to set up a meeting with General Schwarzkopf, the American commander, but he was told this was not possible.

The revolt was doomed; crucial time had been lost. The first city to fall to Saddam Hussein was Basra. Tanks captured the main road and demolished the centres of resistance. Dogs were seen eating dead bodies on the streets.

In the north, Kurds, too, had risen. Saddam Hussein's Republican Guards, who had been pointedly spared by Schwarzkopf, entered the Kurdish town of Sulaimaniya and extinguished the Kurdish resistance.
Saddam Hussein had survived by a whisker; as his troops were celebrating their victory, their ammunition ran out.

Five years later, when Saddam Hussein sent his tanks into another rebellious Kurdish town, Arbil, American aircraft circled the city for twenty minutes and then flew away.

The CIA contingent among the Kurds managed to Iraqi National Congress were rounded up and executed. The CIA contingent among the Kurds managed to flee to safety, while ninety-six members of the CIA-funded Iraqi National Congress were rounded up and executed.

According to Ahmed Chalabi of the INC, tacit American support for the regime was the most significant factor in the suppression of the uprising.

They had made it possible for Saddam to regroup his forces and launch a devastating counterattack with massive firepower on the people.

During war, there was also a lie circulating that the United States allocated billions of dollars' worth of food and medicine for the Iraqi people. The United States did not give a dollar. All humanitarian aid was paid by the Iraqi government, from oil revenues authorised by the UN Security Council.

Kofi Annan, the Secretary General of the United Nations, once criticised the United Nations for holding up seven hundred million dollars' worth of humanitarian supplies.

Most Americans are also unaware that sanctions against Iraq had killed more people than two atomic bombs dropped on Japan, because the media focused on the demonised figure of Saddam Hussein, and presented Iraq as a country of military targets rather than people.

Even before the machinations in the UN Security Council, in October and November 2002, Iraq had already accepted back inspectors of the International Atomic Energy Agency. At the time of writing a new resolution, forced through the Security Council, by the Bush administration's campaign of bribery and coercion, had seen a contingent of weapon inspectors at work in Iraq.

Led by Swedish diplomat, Hans Blix, the inspectors had extraordinary powers, which, for example, required Iraq to confess to possessing equipment, never banned by previous resolutions.

In keeping with US policy, the latest resolution, as it would appear, was designed to fail. In December, then-President Bush announced that Iraq was in breach.

UN Security Resolution 687 says that Iraqi disarmament should be a step towards the goal of establishing in the Middle East a zone free from weapons of mass destruction.

In order words, if Iraq was at the breach and gave up its doomsday weapons, so should Israel. Certainly, if Saddam Hussein was to be indicted by then, so should Ariel Sharon, and so should their Faustian sponsors in the

West, past and present.

A report for UN Secretary-General, written by Professor Bossuyt, a respected authority on international law once believed that sanctions against Iraq were unequivocally illegal under existing human rights law and could raise questions under the Genocide Convention.

The growing body of legal opinion agreed that the new court had a duty, to investigate not only the regime but also the UN bombing and sanctions which had violated the human rights of Iraqi civilians on a vast scale.

It should also investigate who assisted Saddam Hussein's programmes of now-prohibited weapons, including Western governments and companies.

***

For three days, in June 1972, American fighter jets flew fifty-two sorties against Hongai, round the clock. This is believed to be a record, on and off, for six years: one of the heaviest and most concentrated bombings ever inflicted.

The town's other distinction was that it was of the first targets for what was known then as the pellet bomb, the prototype of the cluster bomb. This new weapon discharged hundreds of fragments, many of them shaped like darts.

The more common form of cluster bombs, known as cluster bombs, known in the United States as Rockeyes, were also tested in neighbouring Laos. They exploded into about 160 canisters, or bomblets, half of which lay on the ground, until an animal or person stepped on them, or picked them up, as children often did.

They then exploded. Years later, they continued to kill and maim an estimated twenty thousand people a year in Laos, a tiny country never at war with America, which was bombed as a slideshow to the destruction of Vietnam and Cambodia.

With their legal longevity, cluster bombs are designed purely for terror, as an anti-personnel weapon, to use the military term.

The day Geoffrey Hoon said that the cluster bombs were the best and most effective weapons we have, they were dropped on Gardez, a dirt-prone town in Afghanistan that had long fallen to anti-Taliban forces. The casualty figures are not known. Certainly, seven people in one family of refugees were killed and three were badly injured. They were sheltering in buildings belonging to the United Nations landmine clearing agency, which was destroyed.

The irony went unremarked in the press; cluster bombs are landmines. The crucial difference from those banned under the international treaty is that they are dropped from an aircraft. An estimated seventy thousand American cluster bombs lie unexplored in Afghanistan, already the most landmine country in the world.

Nothing has changed. Not the clusters, which were tested in Vietnam.

Not a shock to the liberal conscience when forced to acknowledge the truth that mass murder, terror, and barbarism are standard practices on our side: only the technology is different.

Not the concealment of true objectives in moral illusions by the richest country on earth using its terrifying military might against the poorest, and in the name of civilisation. Neither has the disregard for peaceful resolution changed. In 1954, US Secretary of State John Foster Dulles walked out of a Geneva conference because the majority has agreed on democratic elections in Vietnam that would unify the north and south of the country. His action ignited a war that took as many as five million lives.

Similarly, in the aftermath of September 11, 2001, the possible ability of a peaceful resolution was sabotaged.

The leaders of Pakistan's two Islamic parties said that they had negotiated Osama bin Laden's extradition to Pakistan, even though the Americans had supplied no evidence with which to prosecute him for the Twin Towers attack.

He was to be held under house arrest in Peshawar. The plan was approved by Bin Laden himself and the Taliban leader, Mullah Omar.

An international tribunal would then hear evidence and decide whether to try him or hand him over to America. A delegation of Islamic clerics from Pakistan, supporters of the Taliban, met Mullah Omar in Kandahar, and told him that Pakistan would plunge into crisis if Osama Bin Laden was not handed over.

Under pressure from Washington, Pakistan's then President Musharraf vetoed the plan, which, said an American official risked a premature collapse of the international effort to capture Bin Laden.

Perhaps, we shall never know if the proposal was genuine or might have been successful.

When the bombing of Afghanistan began, the US and

British governments lied that no peaceful alternative was ever on offer. The bombing of Afghanistan replaced unwanted tribes with preferred tribes.

That both groups are extremists, is beside the point. President Bush once called the occupiers of Kabul, the Northern Alliance as friends.

These are the same people welcomed with kite flying in 1992, who then killed an estimated fifty thousand people in four years of internecine feuding. In 1994 alone, reported New York-based Human Rights Watch, an estimated twenty-five thousand people were killed in Kabul, most of them civilians, in rockets and artillery attacks. One-third of the city was reduced to rubble.

Having tortured and executed hundreds of prisoners of war, as well as looted foreign aid warehouses, the new heroes had quietly reestablished their monopoly over the affairs of the nation, as well as the heroin trade.

Life was meant to be easier for Afghan women, but the *burqa* remained, as remained most of the Taliban laws. Only a third of the children are educated, of these, less than three per cent are girls. Sexual policing has also thrived over time. Fazul Hadi Shinwari, then Chief Justice of the Supreme Court, once said that Taliban's Sharia punishments shall continue, including stoning and amputation.

When then-President Hamid Karzai, installed by Washington ruled, he installed a tribal council that was seen by most Afghans as a sham. During his rule, Karzai was guarded by 46 American Special Forces soldiers and survived one assassination attempt.

His country was stricken, with the arrival of only a fraction of the money promised by its liberators, with which they pledged to build civilian infrastructure.

The Americans dropped ten thousand tonnes of bombs. The United Nations estimates that between fifty to a hundred people were killed by unexploded bombs and landmines every week.

The greater sham is the war on terrorism itself. The search for Osama Bin Laden and his cohorts in the mountains of Afghanistan was a circus spectacle. The American goal is, and always was, the control, through vassals, of former Soviet Central Asia, a region rich in oil, and minerals of great strategic importance to competing powers, Russia and China.

By February 2002, the United States had established permanent military bases in all the Central Asian Republics, and in Afghanistan, whose post-Taliban government was American-approved.

The goal is far wider conquest, military and economic, which was planned during the Second World War, which as then Vice President Dick Cheney believed may not end in our life until the United States has positioned itself as the gatekeeper of the world's remaining oil and gas.

Once the Taliban retreated south from Kabul, Cheney and Defence Secretary Rumsfeld made this clear that America was planning action against forty to fifty countries. Somalia, allegedly a haven for the Islamic cult al-Qaeda, joined Iraq at the top of the list of potential targets.

Rumsfeld disclosed that he had asked the Pentagon to think the unthinkable, after having rejected its post-

Afghanistan options as not radical enough. He did not mention that Somalia and part of the northwestern Indian Ocean are major oil and gas reserves, perhaps as large as the Caspian Sea.

There, too, American companies have staked claims and await the imposition of a pro-Western regime. There is no evidence that al Qaeda has bases in Somalia. The Americans are listening to a clan militia called Rahanwein, supported by and grinding the axe of neighbouring Ethiopia, which has long sought to keep Somalia weak and divided.

September 11 provided Bush's Washington with a remarkable justification. Pakistan's former Foreign Minister, Niaz Niak was told by American officials in mid-July 2001 that military action against Afghanistan would go ahead by the middle of October. Former Secretary of State Colin Powell was then travelling in Central Asia, already gathering support for an anti-Afghanistan war coalition.

For Washington, the real problem with the Taliban was not their human rights violations; these were irrelevant. At first, welcomed by Washington, the Taliban did not have total control of Afghanistan; *mujahedeen* factions held territory in the north. For this reason, to the Americans, the regime lacked stability, and the control required of all clients.

It was this lack of stability that deterred investors from continuing to finance oil and gas pipelines from the Caspian Sea, whose largely untapped fossil fuels of the Caspian Basin have become central, if not critical, to American planning.

In 1998, Dick Cheney, then a consultant on pipelines

to several Central Asian republics told a conference of oil industry executives that he could not think of a time when they had a region emerge as suddenly to become as strategically significant as the Caspian.

Western interest in the Caspian Sea goes back to the era when oil was discovered and exploited for the first time. Near the end of the nineteenth century, Russia fought to keep John R Rockefeller's Standard Oil Company out of Caspian.

Not only America, and the European imperial powers wanted Caspian oilfields. Hitler, in his invasion of Russia, and before running short of fuel and being defeated at Stalingard, planned to take the saving price of Caspian resources, and then drive south, for the even greater prize of Persia and Iraq, as a contemporary journalist, John Rees, has pointed out.

For the West, the existence of the Soviet Union barred the way to oil and gas reserves, whose potential excited constant speculation. The largest inland sea was said, perhaps optimistically, to contain a third of the world's oil and gas reserves.

The most extensive fields are in Kazakhstan and Azerbaijan, with smaller fields in Turkmenistan and Uzbekistan. Following the demise of the Soviet Union, the United States, Russia, China, France, Britain, and Germany have competed in an oil rush, reminiscent of the disordered imperial competition in Africa.

In the 1990s, the United States staked its claim with several demonstrations of its global reach, such as the well-publicised deployment of five hundred paratroopers from the 82nd Airborne Division in North Carolina to the desert of Kazakhstan.

At the time, this was the longest airborne operation in military history and meant that there was no nation on earth where the US could not go, adding the apparent afterthought that the US was concerned with promoting independent, sovereign states that can defend themselves.

President Clinton's Energy Secretary, Bill Richardson once candidly described the Soviet republics as all about America's energy security. Richardson believed that he would like to see them reliant on Western commercial and political investment in the Caspian and that it was very important for them that the pipeline map and the politics came out right.

The pipeline map is critical, as the oil and gas are worthless without the means to carry them to deep-water ports. There are three routes a pipeline could go: through Russia, Iran, or Afghanistan.

For Washington, dependence on Russia is an abomination, and Iran has been the country America has spent more than twenty years isolating.

It was not surprising that, in 1996, when the Taliban took power in Kabul, they found themselves courted by the American oil lobby, with its eye on one of the greatest prizes of the twenty-first century, as the *Daily Telegraph* reported. Oil industry insiders say that the dream of securing a pipeline across Afghanistan is the main reason Pakistan, a close political ally of America, had been so supportive of the Taliban, and why America has quietly acquiesced in its conquest of Afghanistan.

Following September 11, 2001, none was more fervent

in calling for the overthrow of the Taliban than the *Wall Street Journal.*

However, five years earlier, the authentic voice of the American capital had struck an entirely different tone. The Taliban, the paper declared, are the players most capable of achieving peace in Afghanistan. Moreover, their success was crucial to secure Afghanistan as a prime trans-shipment route, for the export of Central Asia's vast oil, gas, and other natural resources.

Not only were the Taliban welcomed by Washington, but Taliban leaders were also flown to Texas, then governed by George W Bush, and entertained in Houston by senior executives of the oil company Unocal (United Oil of California).

According to George Monbiot, the company suggested paying these barbarians fifteen cents for every cubic foot of gas pumped through the land they had conquered. A Clinton administration official commented that Afghanistan would become like Saudi Arabia, an oil colony with no democracy, and the legal persecution of women.

In 1998, Unocal's Vice-President for International Relations John J Maresa told a Congressional inquiry that by 2010, Western companies could increase oil production to 4.5 million barrels a day, an increase of more than five hundred per cent in fifteen years. He appealed for the development of an appropriate investment climate in the region.

By this, he meant that construction of the pipeline proposed across Afghanistan could not begin until a recognised government is in place that has the confidence of governments, lenders, and the company.

He made no mention of the barbaric nature of the regime, or the al Qaeda extremists he was meant to entertain.

When Unocal eventually signed a memorandum of understanding, to build a pipeline from Turkmenistan to Pakistan via Afghanistan, it did so on behalf of a consortium of Enron, Amoco, British Petroleum, Chevron, Exxon, and Mobil.

The dealmakers were Dick Cheney, former Defence Secretary, and future Vice President, James Baker, former Secretary of State, and Brent Scowcroft, former National Security Advisor to the President. All had served in the Cabinet of George Bush Senior.

Bush Senior was a paid consultant to the bin Laden family through the Carlyle Group, which owns sixty-four companies that specialise in oil and gas, aerospace, and weapons. The former president has met the family twice.

The pipeline deal fell through when two American embassies in east Africa were bombed and al-Qaeda was blamed. The frisson between Washington and Taliban had since been revived when Hamid Karzai was president, a former employee of Unocal subsidiary, and the appointment as American Ambassador to Afghanistan of none other than Unocal's John J Maresca.

Post-bombing deals have also been struck with the Caspian's oil republics, all of them sporting appalling human rights records. As the bombing of Afghanistan had gotten underway, Rumsfeld promised tens and billions of dollars to Tajikistan and Uzbekistan, which share nine hundred miles of border with Afghanistan.

The Russians are not happy with this arrangement, believing the republics would move closer to Moscow, as a counterweight to the Americans.

Vladimir Putin's collaboration has won favours in Washington, such as prospects of further strategic arms reductions and the license to proceed with his war on terrorism in Chechnya, where an estimated twenty thousand people have been killed.

The reason Chechnya is so important to Putin is that it is one of the last routes for Caspian Oil. As Russians see it, the deal is that they keep Chechnya and the US gets unprecedented access to Central Asia.

***

Almost after a decade after the 1991 Gulf War, the American photographer Kim Jarecke spoke about censorship by omission in the free press. His was the breath catching a picture of an Iraqi burned to a blackened cinder, petrified at the wheel of his vehicle on the Basra Road where, along with hundreds of others, he was incinerated by American pilots during their 'turkey shoot' of retreating Iraqis and foreign nationals, mostly guest workers, trapped in Kuwait.

The Observer alone published the picture, though not on the front page where it belonged. In the United States, it was suppressed until long after the war was over.

This one image stripped away the propaganda that Desert Storm had been an almost bloodless war. According to Jerecke, no one would touch the photograph. The excuse was that it was too upsetting and people did not want to look at that kind of thing anymore.

The truth was that the whole US press collaborated in keeping silent about the consequences of the Gulf War and who was responsible.

Jean Baudrillard's thesis that the Gulf War did not take place was dismissed at the time as the ramblings of an otherworldly French philosopher. However, as Phil Coles has pointed out, 'his basic claim that what we witnessed was purely a media performance aimed to assert US military authority over the globe was clear enough, and seems just as pertinent now.'

As the media age is often confused with an information age, it is understandable that we have a war by the media. The open and occasionally critical reporting of the Vietnam War was a lesson to Western militarists.

When George Bush Senior invaded Panama, no journalist witnessed the destruction of a swathe of Panama City.

Only later was a pool of reporters allowed limited access, and they were told that General Noriega's men, not helicopter gunships, had torched the slums.

Press conferences became events: arenas for dispensing propaganda such as entertaining videotapes, showing the surgical bombing of alleged military facilities.

What was striking during the Gulf War was how few journalists questioned the truth of these images or enquired about how the tapes were edited. They, like the commentators at home, were in thrall to the very accuracy of new weapons, as the BBC's David Dimbleby excitedly put it.

In fact, less than seven per cent of the weapons used in Desert Storm were smart, as Pentagon admitted long after the war.

Seventy per cent of the 88,550 bombs dropped on Iraq and Kuwait – the equivalent of seven Hiroshima's – missed their targets completely, and many fell in populated areas.

The launch sites of Iraq's Scud missiles were said to have been knocked out. Not one was destroyed. None of this was reported on time. Journalists were lied to and, accepting the lies, passed them on to the public.

The Basra Road, which Kim Jarecke photographed, was only one of many massacres. The others were not reported, having been carried out beyond the scrutiny of the press pool. Unknown to journalists, in the last two days before the ceasefire, American armoured bulldozers were ruthlessly deployed, mostly at night, to bury Iraqis alive in their trenches, including the wounded.

Six months later, *New York Newsday* disclosed that three brigades of the US First Mechanised Infantry Division used snowploughs mounted on tanks and combat earthmovers to bury thousands of Iraqi soldiers – some still alive – in more than seventy miles of trenches.

The only images of this atrocity to be shown on television were used, bizarrely, as a backdrop to a discussion about the reporting of the war on a late-night BBC arts programme, with its participants oblivious to the disturbing scenes on the screen behind them. General Schwarzkopf's policy was that Iraqi dead were not to be counted.

Although, he did provide figures to Congress, indicating that at least a hundred thousand Iraqi soldiers had been killed. But he offered no estimate of civilian causalities.

Shortly before Christmas 1991, the Medical Educational Trust in London published a comprehensive study of casualties. Up to a quarter of a million men, women and children were killed or died as a direct result of the American-led attack on Iraq. This confirmed American and French intelligence estimates of more than two hundred thousand deaths. The sheer level of this killing never entered public consciousness in the West.

When great truths are omitted, myths take their place, and the nature and pattern of great power are never explained to the public. Instead, militarism is presented as a morality play. Once again Blair applied his whitewash saying that whatever faults they had, Britain had been a very strong moral nation with a sense of right and wrong. He further believed that moral fibre would defeat the fanaticism of the extremists and their supporters.

He was not referring to the fanatics who deliberately caused so many deaths in Iraq, Yugoslavia, and Afghanistan.

By any true moral light, the pretence that these crimes did not happen is itself a crime. The Orwellian twist is that crime is justified by its ethical dimension.

Although it has since been abandoned as an embarrassment, an ethical dimension was the ambition ascribed to New Labour's foreign policy by the former Foreign Secretary Robin Cook.

It was, for a while, a brilliant ruse. Instead of putting human rights at the centre of British foreign policy, as Cook promised, the British Government pursued, normal, policies that ignored human rights or fostered their violation.

When an arms business second only in size to that of the United States, Britain continued to sell two-thirds of its lethal weapons and military equipment to governments with appalling human rights records. Its biggest customer is Saudi Arabia, the most extreme Islamic regime on earth, tutors the Taliban and had been home to most of the alleged September 11 hijackers.

An investigation by the National Audit Office into the 20 billion pounds 'Al Yamamah' (The Dove) arms deal, whose report both Conservative and Labour governments refused to release, describes commissions paid on Tornado fighters – 15 million pounds on one aircraft was said to be the going rate.

Britain is the major arms supplier to at least five countries with internal conflict, where the combined death toll runs to almost a million people.

Countries on the verge of war with each other are also clients: for example, India and Pakistan. For twenty years, Britain armed the Indonesian genocidal regime in East Timor.

When Blair's Government came to power, and Cook made his mission statement at Foreign Office, he met two Nobel Prize winners, Bishop Carlos Beto and Jose Ramos Horta, of East Timor. He assured them Britain would not license weapons that might be used for internal repression in their occupied country.

The government's response was to increase arms shipment to Indonesia under the cover of the Official Secrets Act. These included Heckler and Koch machine guns used by General Suharto's special forces in East Timor, who had been identified as the source of the worst human rights abuses, including massacre and torture. On September 11, 2001, when America was being attacked, the Blair Government was hosting arms fair in London's Docklands attended by various human rights cases of abuse, including Saudi Arabia, the spiritual home of al-Qaeda, and the birthplace of Osama bin Laden.

Out of respect for the victims of the Twin Towers atrocity, the annual conference of the Trades Union Congress was curtailed along with sporting fixtures and other public events. The arms fair went ahead. Shortly afterwards, in an interview with David Frost, Blair declared that the way to defeat extremists was to stop people who gave them weapons.

For the British, who invented the modern arms trade, business as usual is an act of faith.

While George Bush was describing an axis of evil, that included Iran, the Blair Government was approving the sale of chemical weapons to Iran, and 25 other countries including Libya, Syria, and Israel.

In the United States, the world's supermarket of weapons, the making and selling of arms is central to any economic boom. The American military-industrial complex is held aloft by arms and other military-related contracts. Forty cents in every tax dollar ends with the Pentagon. War ensures the industry's prosperity.

Following the Gulf War, American arms sales increased by sixty-four per cent. The NATO attack on Yugoslavia resulted in an extra \$17 billion in sales. Following September 11, a boom had been already seen in the weapons business.

The day the stock markets reopened after the attacks, the few companies showing increased value were the military contractors Raytheon, Alliant Tech Systems, Northrop Gruman, and Lockheed Martin.

Lockheed Martin's share value rose by thirty per cent. The company's main plant is in George W Bush's home state of Texas. As governor, Bush tried unsuccessfully to sell the Texas welfare system to Lockheed Martin-owned companies. In 1999, the company had record arms sales of more than $25 billion and received more than $12 billion in Pentagon contracts.

Within six weeks of the Twin Tower attacks, Lockheed Martin had secured the biggest military order in history: a $200 billion contract to develop a fighter aircraft. The aircraft was to be built in Fort Worth, Texas, creating thirty-two thousand new jobs.

The British arms industry has also boomed since September 2001. BAE systems have been selling a forty million-air defence system to Tanzania, one of the world's poorest countries. With a per capita income of $250 a year, half of the population has no clean running water, and one in four children dies before their fifth birthday.

***

ABOUT THE AUTHOR

Naveed Qazi was born and brought up in Srinagar, Kashmir Valley.

He did his bachelor's degree in commerce from the University of Kashmir, and a master's degree in international business from the University of Hertfordshire.

BIBLIOGRAPHY

Warrick, J. 2016. *Black flags: The Rise of ISIS*. London: Corgi Books.

Rashid, Ahmed. 2013. *Pakistan on the Brink: The Future of Pakistan Afghanistan and the West*. London: Penguin.

Pilger, J. 2016. *The New Rulers of the World*. London: Verso.

Brautigam, D. 2011. *The Dragon's Gift: The Real Story of China in Africa*. Oxford: Oxford University Press.

Macaes, Bruno. 2018. *Belt and Road: The Sinews of Chinese Power*. C Hurst and Co Publications Limited

Gallagher, K. 2016. *The China Triangle: Latin America's China Boom and the fate of the Washington Consensus*. New York, NY, United States of America: Oxford University Press.